IMAGES
of America

JEWISH COMMUNITIES OF THE FIVE TOWNS AND THE ROCKAWAYS

IMAGES
of *America*

JEWISH COMMUNITIES
OF THE FIVE TOWNS
AND THE ROCKAWAYS

The Jewish Heritage Society of the Five Towns

ARCADIA
PUBLISHING

Copyright © 2015 by the Jewish Heritage Society of the Five Towns
ISBN 978-1-5316-7810-4

Published by Arcadia Publishing
Charleston, South Carolina

Library of Congress Control Number: 2015933857

For all general information, please contact Arcadia Publishing:
Telephone 843-853-2070
Fax 843-853-0044
E-mail sales@arcadiapublishing.com
For customer service and orders:
Toll-Free 1-888-313-2665

Visit us on the Internet at www.arcadiapublishing.com

This book is dedicated to the men and women who paved the way to create one of the most vibrant Jewish communities in the United States. Their vision and their tenacity transcended bigotry and suspicion, exclusion and distrust. Throughout the years they have learned to build bridges, engage in unity, as well as embrace diversity without compromising on personal principles and ideals. It is their courage and search for the truth that made the Five Towns and outlying areas a rich bastion of Jewish life and education.

This book is also dedicated in loving memory of Arthur Elfenbein, who passed away at the last stages of its production. His camera captured the soul of this community, but his big heart captured its love.

CONTENTS

ACKNOWLEDGMENTS

The Jewish Heritage Society of the Five Towns, a charitable organization, tax exempt under section 501(c)3 of the Internal Revenue Code, was founded through the vision of Rabbi Benjamin Kamenetzky, who was one of the original pioneers of the Orthodox Jewish community of the Five Towns. At the 50th anniversary of the founding of Yeshiva of South Shore in 2006, Rabbi Kamenetzky commissioned a group of volunteers to collect and organize photographs, newspaper clippings, and other artifacts that documented the history of the growth of the community. That collection grew through the efforts of dozens of men and women, institutions, and organizations who were eager to share their wealth of knowledge and their cherished memories. Among them, we acknowledge, first and foremost, Dr. Shneur Leiman, a true scholar and historian with a broad-based, yet detailed knowledge of the history of the Jewish communities of the Rockaways and, more importantly, of the Hebrew Institute of Long Island, where his father, Rabbi Harold I. Leiman, served as principal. His graciousness in allowing for the open and unrestricted dissemination of material that he worked tirelessly in culling is a true sign of the graciousness inherent in his essence. He has been a friend and mentor in this project. Rabbi Mordechai Kamenetzky has been an invaluable source for photographs and information. A native of the Five Towns, he cherishes the chance to recount stories and anecdotes relating to its history. Richard Hagler of the Hebrew Academy of Long Beach, Ruben Maron of the Hebrew Academy of the Five Towns and Rockaways, and Danny Frankel and Paul Hanau of Young Israel of Woodmere provided pictures. The unofficial photographer of all Woodmere activities in the late 1960s, Arthur Elfenbein, also provided photographs for this book. Congregation Shaaray Tefila's administration, led by Sam Davies, was very helpful in providing pictures and information regarding their synagogue. We also want to thank the Long Island Divisions of the Queens Library and Hofstra University for their input and allowing us to use photographs of landmarks that helped the community flourish.

The Jewish Heritage Society of the Five Towns would also like to thank Nassau County executive Edward P. Mangano and Nassau County legislator Howard J. Kopel for their support and encouragement of this project and all the projects of the Society. The Lev Tov Challenge and Keren Maasim Tovim Foundations, headed by Avraham P. Berkowitz, continue to play a key role in all our efforts to transmit our heritage, and we cannot thank them enough. A special thanks to the Lehmann, Eisner, Langer, Hirshaut, Maidenbaum, Blumenthal, and Gut families who have been supporters of the Jewish Heritage Society's mission to preserve the history and heritage of our community. Thanks also to the Rappaport family for their support.

Unless otherwise noted, images appear courtesy of the Jewish Heritage Society of the Five Towns. For further information about the Jewish Heritage Society of the Five Towns, please visit our website at www.jhsft.org or e-mail us at info@jhsft.org.

Look for our upcoming publication *Flowers in the Desert: The Story of the Growth and Development of the Five Towns Orthodox Jewish Community*, a coffee table book in full color, depicting the full story of the major personalities and institutions that paved the path for one of the largest and most influential Orthodox communities in the United States.

INTRODUCTION

A picture is worth a thousand words.

The Jewish Heritage Society of the Five Towns is proud to present a treasure trove of images that depict the formative years of the Five Towns and Far Rockaway area.

This image collection is unique, as it depicts an ongoing story—one that continues to emerge and develop, like a child growing stronger. Jewish life in many American cities is just part of the past; however, the Five Towns and Rockaways support the opposite. Jewish life and customs continue to thrive.

The images in this collection are from a time when Orthodox Jewish life in the Five Towns was shaky at best, and the images captured within this book tell of the perseverance that led these communities to flourish, embodying traditional Jewish life within the modernity of life in the United States. Indeed, many communities in Brooklyn or Rockland County are also vibrant with Hasidic Orthodoxy, and they, too, emerged from the embers of the Holocaust. However, the Five Towns has maintained a certain modernity that is able to blend American life with hundreds of families who are strongly committed to the traditional values and observances as proscribed in the Code of Jewish Law yet are professionals with modern American lives. It took the concerted efforts of devoted men and women to create a community that would be committed to old values while adapting to American life.

Most of the photographs came from a treasure trove gathered by Rabbi Benjamin Kamenetzky over the nearly 60 years he has been living in Woodmere. At the time of his arrival, it was difficult to find 10 men who would want to join a minyan. Only one coeducational day school existed in Far Rockaway, and the pioneers of Orthodoxy wanted to preserve their strong commitment to tradition and Jewish rituals by creating a community with many more choices. The plan worked, people kept their commitment to Judaism, and the rate of assimilation was far less than other communities across Long Island and suburban areas in the northeast whose Jewish populations dwindle through attrition and assimilation.

Rabbi Mordechai Kamenetzky, a native of the Five Towns who has children and grandchildren, loves to point to the streets packed with strollers and children on a Jewish holiday and reminisce: "I was the only boy who wore a yarmulke within six blocks of my house." His children and grandchildren look at him in wonder and are unable to comprehend that indeed there was such a time in the Five Towns. It is a sad contrast to towns across the United States that once had 9 or 10 kosher butchers and dozens of synagogues, though today not even a single piece of kosher meat or a minyan can be located in those towns.

People who have heart and soul—but not necessarily cameras—build communities. This book is not a mere narrative of history; the images in this collection are specific to a certain period of time and a criteria established by the publishers of this series. And where there were no images, it would be almost impossible to tell a story, and thus, many people and institutions may not have been included in this volume. Sometimes, we were only able to avail ourselves of only a few pictures that depicted major institutions, such as the White Shul, whereas other institutions had many more.

This volume focuses primarily on institutions that began in the 1960s or earlier. Unfortunately, we did not include every school or synagogue if we did not have proper photographs for them. A large collection that belonged to Torah Academy for Girls, which began in the early 1960s, was lost during Hurricane Sandy, and we were not able to obtain pictures from the era that fell into Arcadia's criteria. Yeshiva Darchei Torah, founded in the early 1970s, actually began in Shaaray Tefila. Even though it is now perhaps one of the largest and most influential schools in the Far Rockaway area, we were unable to get pictures of its founding years, and the only ones available were of its modern campus that now occupies what was once the El Roche complex that had become Hebrew Institute of Long Island (HILI).

Yeshiva of Far Rockaway was another early institution not covered in the book. Rabbi Nathan Bulman, who moved to Israel where he lived until his passing in 2002, was a powerhouse of a rabbi who served at the Young Israel of Far Rockaway and founded that school, which is still thriving under the leadership of Rabbi Yechiel Perr.

The following were omitted from the book due to lack of space, time-era criteria, and the black-and-white imagery specific to this series: Agudath Israel of Long Island, Agudath Israel of West Lawrence, Agudath Israel of the Five Towns, Beis Medrash Ateres Yisroel founded by Rabbi Avraham Blumenkranz, and Rabbi Shmelke Rubin's shteeble. Since the mid-1980s, the Five Towns has seen synagogues and yeshivas appear on almost every street corner, and we apologize for not including them.

The Sephardic community has also burgeoned over the last 20 years, and there are quite a number of synagogues that cater to the unique customs and *nusach* (order of prayer) of those particular communities. The large Sephardic Temple on Branch Boulevard, under the longtime leadership of Rabbi Arnold Marans, was the only Sephardic synagogue that met the time period criteria. It is unique to most Sephardic synagogues, as it allows for mixed seating. The liberal nature of that rule did not appeal to the young Sephardic families who have moved into the neighborhood over the last 20 years, and thus, many new synagogues were opened to cater to their desires. However, they were established recently and did not fit the criteria for entry.

When walking into a beautifully crafted and decorated home, some people wonder, "Who were the builders? Who placed these items here?" Others just enjoy what they have, forgetting that it took the hard work of builders, architects, and planners in making this home. This book will help the new arrivals to know about the area's planners, architects, and builders.

One

ICONIC LANDMARKS

Seagirt Boulevard (formerly Avenue) spans the South Shore of the Rockaway Peninsula and stretches approximately two miles from the Rockaway Freeway in Edgemere, New York, until the Nassau County border at the Atlantic Beach Bridge. Only a short walk from the Atlantic Ocean, Seagirt Boulevard was a main thoroughfare that was home to many of the iconic Jewish hotels and institutions of the Rockaways. (Courtesy of the Leiman Collection.)

CENTRAL AVENUE OFF CEDARHURST AVENUE, CEDARHURST, L. I.

Central Avenue Cedarhurst was once the main suburban thoroughfare of the Five Towns, beginning at Franklin Avenue in Woodmere and continuing west approximately 3.5 miles, through Woodmere, Cedarhurst, Lawrence, and Inwood until Mott Avenue in Far Rockaway. Today, many of the stores that occupy Central Avenue are closed on the Jewish Sabbath in regard to the large Orthodox population. (Courtesy of the Leiman Collection.)

The meeting of Central and Mott Avenues remains an iconic corner in Far Rockaway. The triangular-shaped National Bank, built in 1912, and the firehouse across the street were icons of the community. In the late 1960s, a building next door to the bank was purchased to house Sh'or Yoshuv, a Talmudical institute. The bank is now a medical office building. The firehouse still remains. Sh'or Yoshuv has since moved to the Lawrence–Far Rockaway border on a multiacre campus. (Courtesy of the Leiman Collection.)

Borenstein's Redstone Hotel at Seagirt Avenue and Beach Twelfth Street was a famous kosher resort in the Far Rockaway area, especially during the 1930s and 1940s. In 1947, Mr. Borenstein bought and operated the nearby Seagirt Hotel on Seagirt Avenue and Beach Fourteenth Street. In 1948, he sold the Seagirt Hotel to David Hirsch, who operated the hotel throughout the 1950s as a very popular and successful kosher resort known as Hirsch's Hotel. In the 1950s, the building was sold to the Hebrew Institute of Long Island (HILI) and, in an attempt to provide income for HILI, Simon Cohen, HILI's legendary chairman of the board, transformed the hotel into a residential hotel for senior citizens. It was called HILI Manor. The back of the card states, "Open all year, strictly kosher cuisine, social programs and entertainment." (Courtesy of the Leiman Collection.)

HOTEL GENADEEN—LAPIDUS BROS. PROPS.—271 BEACH 19th STREET, FAR ROCKAWAY, N. Y.

The Genadeen Hotel opened in 1922 at 271 Beach Nineteenth Street. The Lapidus brothers owned and operated this premier kosher hotel and hosted many rabbinic conferences and conventions, including that of the Union of Orthodox Rabbis of America and the Agudath Israel of America. In 1950, the Far Rockaway Jewish community held a reception at the Genadeen Hotel for the chief rabbi of Israel, Rabbi Isaac Herzog, that was attended by many prominent dignitaries, including Rabbi Shimshon Zelig Fortman of the White Shul in Far Rockaway, Rabbi Emanuel Rackman of Shaaray Tefila in Far Rockaway, Rabbi Charles B. Chavel of Shaarey Zedek in Edgemere, and Rabbi Eugene Cohen of Derech Emunah in Arverne. In the fall of 1951, Rabbi Raphael Pelcovitz began his tenure as rabbi of the White Shul. He resided at the Genadeen Hotel until he was able to acquire a home and move his family to Far Rockaway. (Courtesy of the Leiman Collection.)

The Commercial Cable Company building was constructed in 1912 on Beach Seventeenth Street near New Haven Avenue. It processed telegrams to and from Europe. As the use of cables in order to convey information dwindled, the building was put up for sale. In the 1960s, Yeshiva Iyyun Ha-Talmud, under the leadership of Rabbi Abba Berman, acquired it. This was the first institution of higher learning in the Five Towns–Far Rockaway area. The Yeshiva Iyyun Ha-Talmud ultimately moved to Jerusalem, and in 1985 the building was torn down. The last occupant before its demolition was Yeshiva Darchei Torah, established in 1972. (Courtesy of the Leiman Collection.)

The Cedarhurst Firehouse, an iconic building on the corner of Washington and Central Avenues, was built in 1884 and still remains as a landmark in the Five Towns. It straddles the Cedarhurst-Lawrence border and serves as a center for community activity. It is next door to the Hebrew Academy of the Five Towns and Rockaway (HAFTR), which is an elementary school; down the block from Congregation Beth Sholom; and across the street from Mesivta Ateres Yaakov, making it a comforting landmark. Today, members of the Jewish community are involved as volunteer firefighters in both the Lawrence-Cedarhurst and Woodmere Fire Departments.

SAINT JOSEPH'S HOSPITAL — FAR ROCKAWAY, NEW YORK

St. Joseph's Hospital was built in 1904 by the Roman Catholic Church—specifically, Bishop Charles E. McDonnell and the Sisters of St. Joseph—and serviced the entire area stretching west to Edgemere and east to Hewlett, Long Island. It had 48 beds, but when the population swelled in the summer months, the sisters added beds that were sheltered with tents. Patients who could afford it were charged $1 a day. In 1976, Episcopal Health Services, Inc., assumed stewardship of the facility, renaming it St. John's Episcopal Hospital. It still maintains a Jewish chaplain and affords kosher meals for Jewish patients. (Courtesy of the Leiman Collection.)

St. Joseph's Hospital, Far Rockaway, L. I.

Brooklyn Jewish Home for Convalescents

The Brooklyn Jewish Home for Convalescents was founded in Brooklyn in 1921. It moved into its new $750,000 quarters at 609 Beach Ninth Street in 1948. Here, over several decades, thousands of Jews would come to convalesce after hospitalizations that left them too ill to resume the burdens of everyday life. A minyan, led by Rabbi Daniel Meyers, a colorful Torah activist who devoted his life to Jewish causes in the Far Rockaway area and beyond, served the needs of the convalescents and the community. (Courtesy of the Leiman Collection.)

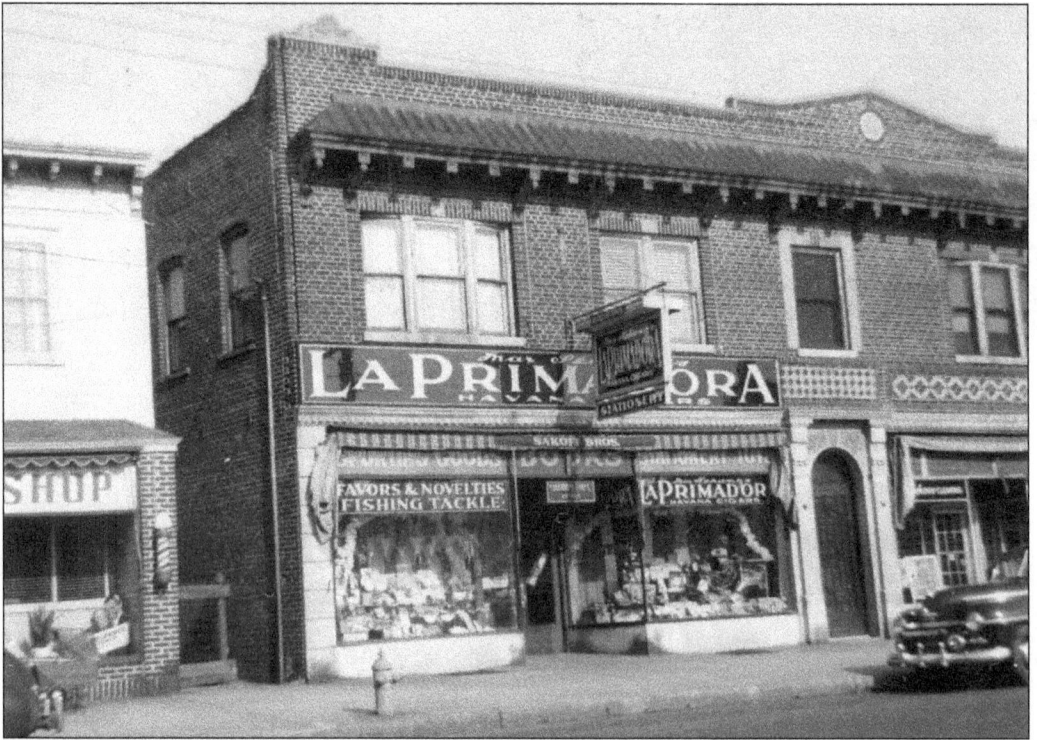

Cedarhurst Avenue runs for about 1.5 miles through the town of Cedarhurst. It begins in Cedarhurst at Peninsula Boulevard and continues until the village of Lawrence, intersecting Central Avenue through the main shopping district. Most recently the village of Lawrence changed Cedarhurst Avenue's name to Briarwood Avenue at the Lawrence Border. Sakoff Brothers stationery and toy store was a prominent icon on Cedarhurst Avenue; its old building is pictured above. For more than 70 years, it sold sundries from cigars to stationery. In the late 1960s, it moved across the street and focused primarily on toys. The original home has since become a fitness club and a kosher restaurant next door.

Two

SYNAGOGUES AND RABBIS

Shaaray Tefila was founded in the early 1900s by a group of 19 men who organized a synagogue whose purpose was to combine traditional Orthodox Judaism with modern American ideas. They wanted to attract and hold the younger generation by its dignity and decorum and beauty of service and to provide a proper Jewish instruction for children. Services were held in the Masonic Temple near the corner of Mott and Central Avenues in Far Rockaway. It was incorporated officially as Congregation "Gates of Prayer" in 1914. At the time, a Hebrew school was established, with Rabbi Benjamin A. Lichter serving as principal. It served as a synagogue, Hebrew school, and Jewish center. The new building, depicted above, was dedicated in 1915 on the day preceding Rosh Hashana, September 8. An additional structure, known as the center building, was dedicated on March 15, 1925. A fire destroyed the main building in 1969, and the congregation then held services in the center building. In 1977, the congregation moved less than a mile eastward to its present home on Central Avenue in Lawrence. (Courtesy of the Leiman Collection.)

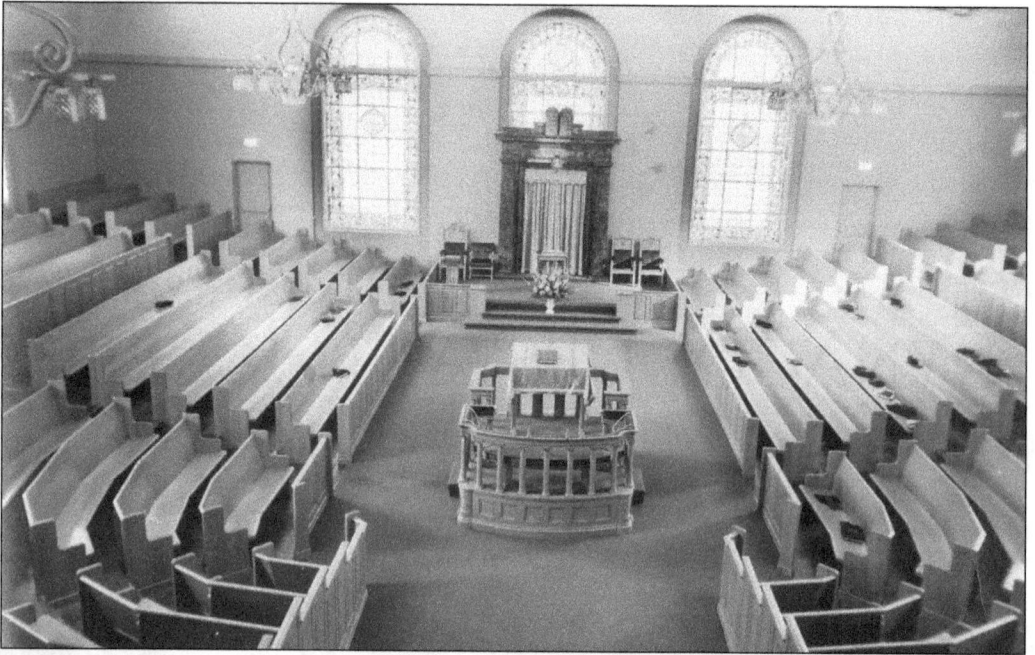

In 1952, construction began to enlarge and beautify the interior of the Shaaray Tefila sanctuary. On August 29, 1953, Shaaray Tefila dedicated the new sanctuary in a service led by the presiding Rabbi Emanuel Rackman, as well as former Rabbi Norman Salit and Rabbi Dr. Samuel Belkin, president of Yeshiva University. The splendid interior of Congregation Shaaray Tefila contained a ceiling with four domes that provided indirect lighting. There was a Star of David in the center. The pews were made of Appalachian-grown honey-colored oak wood. There was lush carpeting and an unusual seating arrangement patterned after the Spanish and Portuguese synagogue. Below is a picture of the dedication ceremony. (Courtesy of Congregation Shaaray Tefila and the Long Island Collection at Hofstra University.)

Rabbi Emanuel Rackman (June 24, 1910–December 1, 2008) was an American Modern Orthodox rabbi who held pulpits in major congregations. He graduated from the Marsha Stern Talmudical Academy in 1927 as his class valedictorian and was ordained at Yeshiva University in 1934. He earned a bachelor's degree from Columbia University in 1931, a bachelor's of laws degree in 1933, and a doctorate of philosophy from Columbia in 1953. Rabbi Rackman practiced law for nine years and served as a chaplain during World War II, where his experiences with survivors of the Holocaust influenced his decision to pursue the rabbinate. Rackman began serving as rabbi of Congregation Shaaray Tefila, then in Far Rockaway, Queens, in 1947. He was granted a lifetime contract in 1952 but accepted a position to succeed Rabbi Immanuel Jakobovits as rabbi of the Fifth Avenue Synagogue in Manhattan in 1967. In addition to congregational leadership, Rabbi Rackman was president of the New York Board of Rabbis and the Rabbinical Council of America as well as Bar-Ilan University. (Courtesy of Congregation Shaaray Tefila.)

This photograph was taken at the dedication ceremony of Congregation Shaaray Tefila. From left to right are Gerson J. Bernstein, the president of the congregation; Rabbi Dr. Samuel Belkin, the president of Yeshiva University; and Rabbi Rackman. Dr. Belkin was the featured speaker at the dedication ceremony. (Courtesy of Congregation Shaaray Tefila.)

Rabbi Rackman was known for his gentle-style oratory. He was a gifted, eloquent spokesman on behalf of Israel and social justice. He is depicted here speaking at an unidentified fundraising dinner. To his left is Rabbi Irving Miller, Rabbi Rackman's predecessor at Congregation Shaaray Tefila and the rabbi at Congregation Sons of Israel. To his right are Nathan Boriskin and Rabbi Benjamin Kamenetzky.

Rabbi Rackman was involved in the Jewish community beyond the scope of his pulpit at Congregation Shaaray Tefila. He is pictured here second from left, testing students at Yeshiva of South Shore, the first boys' yeshiva in the Five Towns, together with Rabbi Benjamin Kamenetzky (right) and the first-grade Hebrew teacher (left).

In 1967, at the age of 57, Rabbi Emanuel Rackman was appointed the spiritual leader of the prominent Fifth Avenue Synagogue in Manhattan. He became an outspoken advocate of a more liberal form of Modern Orthodox Judaism, introducing innovations and ideas that were controversial to his more traditional colleagues. He was an advocate for the plight of women denied *gittin* (religious divorces) by their husbands. He accepted prestigious positions in various institutions of higher learning, serving as provost of Yeshiva University and as head of Jewish Studies at the City University of New York in 1971. In 1977, he became the first American president of Bar-Ilan University in Israel. Rabbi Rackman passed away in December 2008 at the age of 98. (Courtesy of Congregation Shaaray Tefila.)

Rabbi Walter S. Wurzburger
Appointed New Spiritual Leader

After months of diligent effort by a committee under the chairmanship of Mr. Jacob Marrus, Congregation Shaaray Tefila is proud to announce that Rabbi Walter S. Wurzburger has accepted the position. Rabbi Wurzburger comes to us from Toronto, where since 1953 he has served as Rabbi of Shaarei Shomayim Congregation, the leading Orthodox Synagogue in Canada. An acknowledged scholar and teacher, Rabbi Wurzburger is the editor of TRADITION, a distinguished Journal of Orthodox Jewish thought.

He is a graduate of Yeshiva University, 1943 (B.A. Magna Cum Laude), Harvard University, 1946 (M.A.) Harvard University, 1951 (Ph. D.)

Rabbi Wurzburger has held many positions of leadership in various Jewish organizations and is the author of numerous studies in Jewish philosophy and theology and a frequent contributor to professional journals. He is married to the former Naomi C. Rabinovitz, a graduate of Radcliffe College and of the Hebrew Teachers College in Boston. They have three sons: Benjamin, Myror and Joshua.

Rabbi Walter S. Wurzbur...

Rabbi Walter Wurzburger succeeded Rabbi Emanuel Rackman at Congregation Shaaray Tefila in 1968 and led the congregation until 1994. He was a devoted student of Rabbi Joseph B. Soloveitchik and a philosopher and scholar in his own right. A native of Munich, he immigrated to the United States in 1938 and received his bachelor's degree and rabbinical ordination at Yeshiva University, where he taught philosophy from 1967, until the year of his passing. He was considered one of the most intelligent of the Modern Orthodox rabbinate, according to Dr. Norman Lamm, president of Yeshiva University. For 26 years, he was an editor of *Tradition*, an Orthodox journal, and the author of myriad scholarly essays and articles. Rabbi Wurzburger was active in interfaith relations and worked arduously to bridge the gap of what is known as interdenominational Jewry. Pictured above is the press release issued by Shaaray Tefila announcing his appointment. (Courtesy of Congregation Shaaray Tefila.)

Rabbi Walter Wurzburger was a student of Yeshiva University, and his deep ties and gratitude to that institution led him to advocate on its behalf in the Five Towns communities. He is shown here (second from left) with Congressman Herbert Tenzer and other lay leaders at a fundraiser for Yeshiva University. Congressman Tenzer is standing next to rabbi Wurzburger and is proudly holding a Yeshiva University brochure titled "Torah in the 70's." (Courtesy of Congregation Shaaray Tefila.)

Rabbi Wurzburger is shown presenting a Certificate of Award to Rabbi Ephraim Rubin, a longtime resident of the Far Rockaway area and assistant to many of the rabbinical leaders of Congregation Shaaray Tefila. Cherished by countless families for more than half a century, Rabbi Rubin was the foremost mohel in the area. On the far left is the synagogue's cantor, Avram Davis. (Courtesy of Congregation Shaaray Tefila.)

On January 3, 1969, almost 60 years after its construction, a disastrous fire raged through the sanctuary of Congregation Shaaray Tefila, destroying the entire interior of the building. The landmark center of Orthodox Jewish life in Far Rockaway, Queens, was left a smoldering ruin by a fire that burned unreported for at least 35 minutes. A crew of 120 firefighters responded to the three-alarm blaze but could not save the roof from collapsing into the building. Though the main damage was to the sanctuary, devoted congregants who braved potential peril saved the Torah scrolls. Even though it was, at first suspect, arson was eventually ruled out by authorities. (Courtesy of Congregation Shaaray Tefila.)

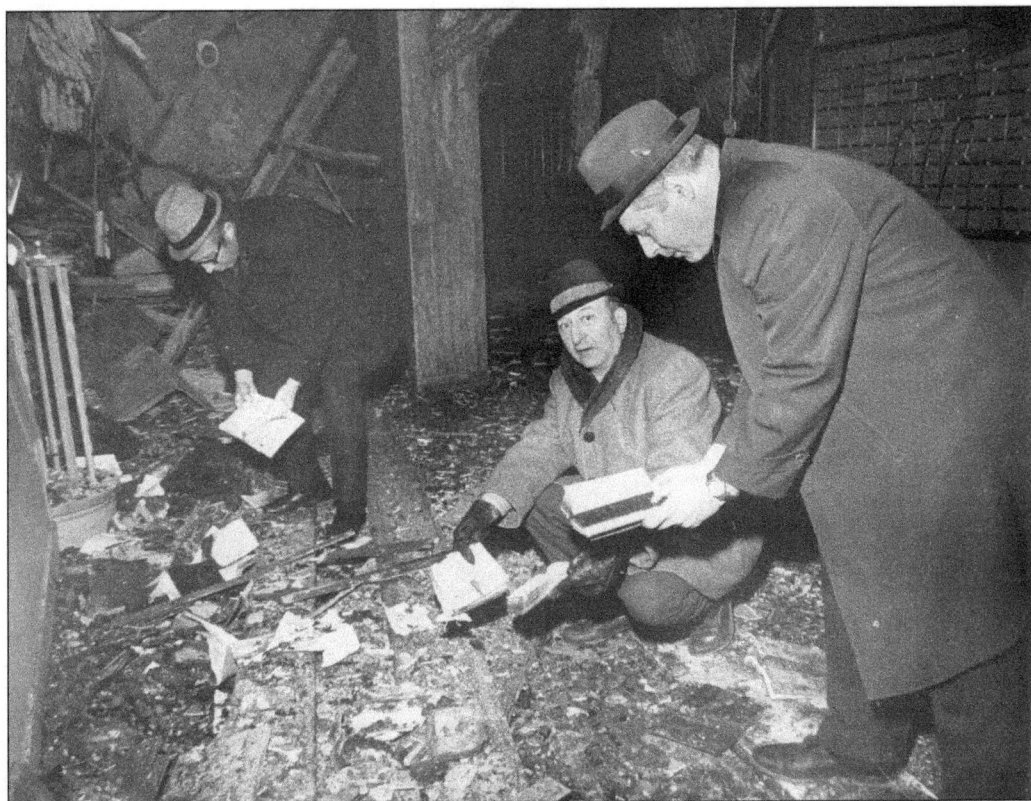

The salvage operation was broad based among the entire community. Jews and non-Jews, blacks and whites, came together to salvage and afford proper last rites to the ruined holy books and to prepare them for the traditional burial. After weeks of extensive communal efforts, the holy books received a proper burial, and the synagogue relocated to the center building until the building of the new synagogue in Lawrence. Pictured above from left to right are Arthur Rogers, Emanuel Lassar, and Rabbi Wurzburger. (Courtesy of Congregation Shaaray Tefila.)

On January 23, 1977, more than eight years after the fire, under a large tent on its newly acquired property in Lawrence, Congregation Shaaray Tefila held a ground-breaking ceremony for its new synagogue. Seen above are, from left to right, Cantor Yitzchok Freund, who continues to serve the congregation to this day; Irwin Selevan; and Congressman John Wydler, who represented the 5th Congressional District from 1973 to 1981. Below, the building's frame is seen only a few months after the initial ground breaking. (Courtesy of Congregation Shaaray Tefila.)

RECORD UJA DINNER RAISES $80,000

Shown here (from left) Harry Walker, Dinner Chairman, Rabbi Walter Wurzburger presenting scroll to Irwin Selevan, Guest of Honor and Emanuel Lassar, President.

Shaaray Tefila remained at the forefront of many communal and Zionist causes for many years. As strong supporters of United Jewish Appeal (UJA) and Israel Bonds, fundraisers were held at the synagogue to support those causes. In the above photograph, Rabbi Wurzburger is shown presenting an award to Irwin Selevan, the guest of honor at a UJA dinner. From left to right are Harry Walker, dinner chairman; Rabbi Wurzburger; Irwin Selevan; and Emanuel Lassar, president. (Courtesy of Congregation Shaaray Tefila.)

Rabbi Shlomo Goren, the chief military rabbi in Israel and eventually the chief rabbi of Israel, visited Shaaray Tefila shortly before the Six-Day War in order to promote support for the State of Israel. Rabbi Goren (right) is shown here together with Rabbi Isaac Freilich, chairman of Israel Bonds. (Courtesy of Congregation Shaaray Tefila.)

CONGREGATION SHAARAY TEFILA

DEDICATION EXERCISES

12 30 PM

THE RABBI'S QUILL

COMMEMORATIVE ANTHOLOGY
OF "RABBI'S MESSAGES"
IN THE SCROLL 1968 – 1994

SPECIAL EDITION
SEFER TORAH COMMEMORATION

IN MEMORY OF
RABBI WALTER S. WURZBURGER ז״ל

MAY 2003

CONGREGATION SHAARAY TEFILA
LAWRENCE, NEW YORK

RABBI WALTER S. WURZBURGER

Rabbi Walter and Naomi Wurzburger are seen standing joyously in front of the announcement board that graced the new location of the synagogue on Central Avenue. The sign announces the dedication ceremonies that were to take place on March 16, 1980. The rabbi and rebbitzin went on to serve the congregation for another 14 years until their retirement in 1994. He passed away in April 2002 at the age of 82. The following year, the congregation published a volume of essays under the title of *The Rabbi's Quill*, a mere morsel of the prolific amount of literature and scholarly works that Rabbi Wurzburger had authored during his distinguished career. (Courtesy of Congregation Shaaray Tefila.)

The Temple Israel, Far Rockaway, N. Y.

What is known as the "White Shul" was originally Temple Israel, a Reform synagogue, constructed in 1930 in Far Rockaway. Temple Israel later moved to new quarters on Central Avenue in Lawrence and sold the building to Congregation Knesseth Israel, an Orthodox congregation that was founded in Far Rockaway in 1922. Congregation Knesseth Israel soon became widely known as White Shul due to the white-frame Colonial structure that then served as its synagogue building. In 1964, Congregation Knesseth Israel moved into its present quarters at Empire Avenue and Sage Street. It is the first synagogue west of the Nassau County border and has served as a center for Jewish activity on both educational and social levels for nine decades. (Courtesy of the Leiman Collection.)

Rabbi Shimshon Zelig HaKohen Fortman (1895–1951) was a Lithuanian rabbi who originally had served as the rabbi in the towns of Kopatkevichi and Osipovichi in Belarus (White Russia). He headed a yeshiva near Slutsk, Lithuania, prior to World War I. Rabbi Fortman was known as a preeminent interpreter of Torah and master orator. Upon arrival in the United Sates, he was appointed rabbi of Congregation Knesseth Israel of Far Rockaway. Rabbi Fortman passed away on 27 Shvat, 5711 (February 3, 1951). Pictured below is his tombstone; it states that Rabbi Fortman served lovingly for 32 years in communities in Russia and in Far Rockaway. Rabbi Fortman had four daughters. Two of them were married to prominent rabbis who helped mold the emerging American Orthodox Jewish community: Rabbi Moshe Sherer, the president of Agudath Israel of America; and Rabbi David Hollander, rabbi of the Mount Eden Jewish Center, president of the Rabbinical Council of America, and a powerful advocate and spokesman for Orthodox Jewry. (Courtesy of the Sherer family and kevorim.com.)

Rabbi Raphael "Ralph" Pelcowitz assumed the position of rabbi of Congregation Knesseth Israel after the passing of Rabbi Fortman in 1951 and was a key contributor to the growth of the Orthodox Jewish community of Far Rockaway and the environs. Born in Canton, Ohio, Rabbi Pelcovitz initially studied in local public schools before continuing at the Hevron Yeshiva in Jerusalem; he was ordained at Yeshiva Torah Vodaath. During his long and successful career, he has taught, guided, and inspired thousands of men, women, and children. He is the author of many scholarly works as well as guides to practical living, the latest of which was authored together with his son David, a renowned psychologist in private practice.

Rabbi Pelcowitz was well known for his brilliant oratory skills and often graced the podium of major community events. Above, he is pictured at the podium addressing the crowd gathered at the ground-breaking ceremony of Yeshiva of South Shore. From left to right are, including those seated in rear, (first row) Congressman Herbert Tenzer; Rabbi Benjamin Kamenetzky, dean of Yeshiva of South Shore; Louis Goldwyn, president of Yeshiva of South Shore; Rabbi Isaac Schmidman, dean of Yeshiva Toras Chaim of East New York; Rabbi Yaakov Kamenetzky, dean of Yeshiva Torah Vodaath; David Usdan; unidentified; and William Janowitz.

Pictured on April 8, 2009, congregants of Knesseth Israel stand in front of the synagogue and recite the "Birkat HaChama," a blessing made once every 28 years commemorating the beginning of a 28-year solar cycle.

In 1928, a group of religious and committed individuals organized a synagogue to be known as "Congregation Derech Yosher, Way of Righteousness to advance the cause of traditional and Orthodox Judaism . . . to promote Jewish education . . . to join hands with local and national causes for the betterment of our community . . . and to help rebuild our homeland." At a special meeting in January 1945, a plan to erect a building of refinement and beauty (pictured) was formulated for a place "where we can worship with dignity—where our children will be taught—where men and women may enjoy community affairs together." Because of the war effort, the name was changed to "Beth Sholom, House of Peace." (Courtesy of Congregation Beth Sholom.)

Albert B. Joffe Laying Cornerstone at Ceremonies Held September 17, 1950. With Mr. Joffe (l. to r.), Hon. Russell Sprague, George Fischbein, Herbert Tenzer and Rabbi Klaperman.

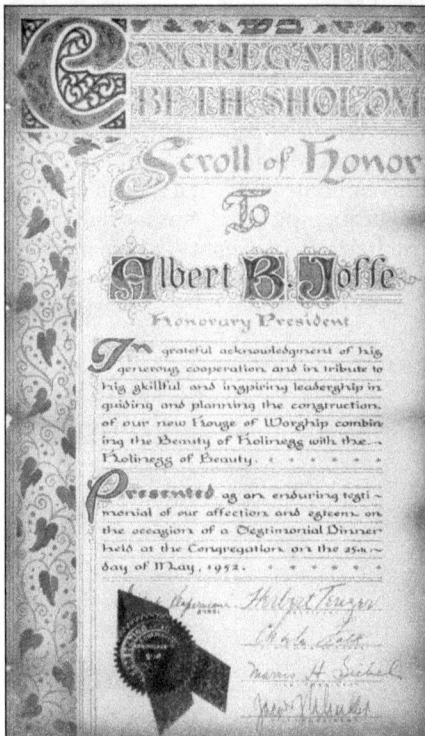

At the 1950 cornerstone-laying ceremony of the new building for Congregation Beth Sholom, Albert Joffe is seen with a trowel together with Nassau County executive Russel Sprague, George Fischbein, Herbert Tenzer, and Rabbi Gilbert Klaperman. It took arduous work, and the building fund committee was constantly at work striving relentlessly to reach the goal. Under careful leadership, intelligent guidance, and liberal assistance of Pres. Albert B. Joffe, the building was finally completed. Albert Joffe was honored in May 1952 for all his efforts in inspiring, planning, fundraising, and executing the completion of the beautiful edifice, the first Orthodox synagogue of its kind in the Five Towns. (Both, courtesy of Congregation Beth Sholom.)

In 1949, ground was broken for the new Beth Sholom building, and in 1950, services were held in the new home (pictured) on Broadway and Washington Avenue in Lawrence. Renovated numerous times, the beautiful edifice stands today as a vibrant center for Jewish study, prayer, and daily activity in Jewish life. (Courtesy of Congregation Beth Sholom.)

From its founding, Congregation Beth Sholom saw several rabbis, including Rabbi Saul Baily and Rabbi Robert Marcus. Rabbi Gilbert Klaperman served the longest tenure—from 1950 until today—at Beth Sholom, where he serves as rabbi emeritus. Rabbi Klaperman, the consummate rabbi and orator, received *smicha* (ordination) from Dr. Samuel Belkin and Rabbi Joseph B. Soloveitchik. A native of Harlem, New York, he served as the rabbi of a Hillel Center in Canada, and as a rabbi in Charleston, South Carolina, before his appointment to rabbi of Beth Sholom. He is a cosmopolitan leader with a world vision who has met heads of state, including Kennedy, Nixon, Khrushchev, and Pope John Paul II, the latter two in an effort to open channels of emigration for Soviet Jews and to have the Vatican recognize the State of Israel, which it did. He has served as president of the Rabbinical Council of America and on the New York Board of Rabbis. (Courtesy of Congregation Beth Sholom.)

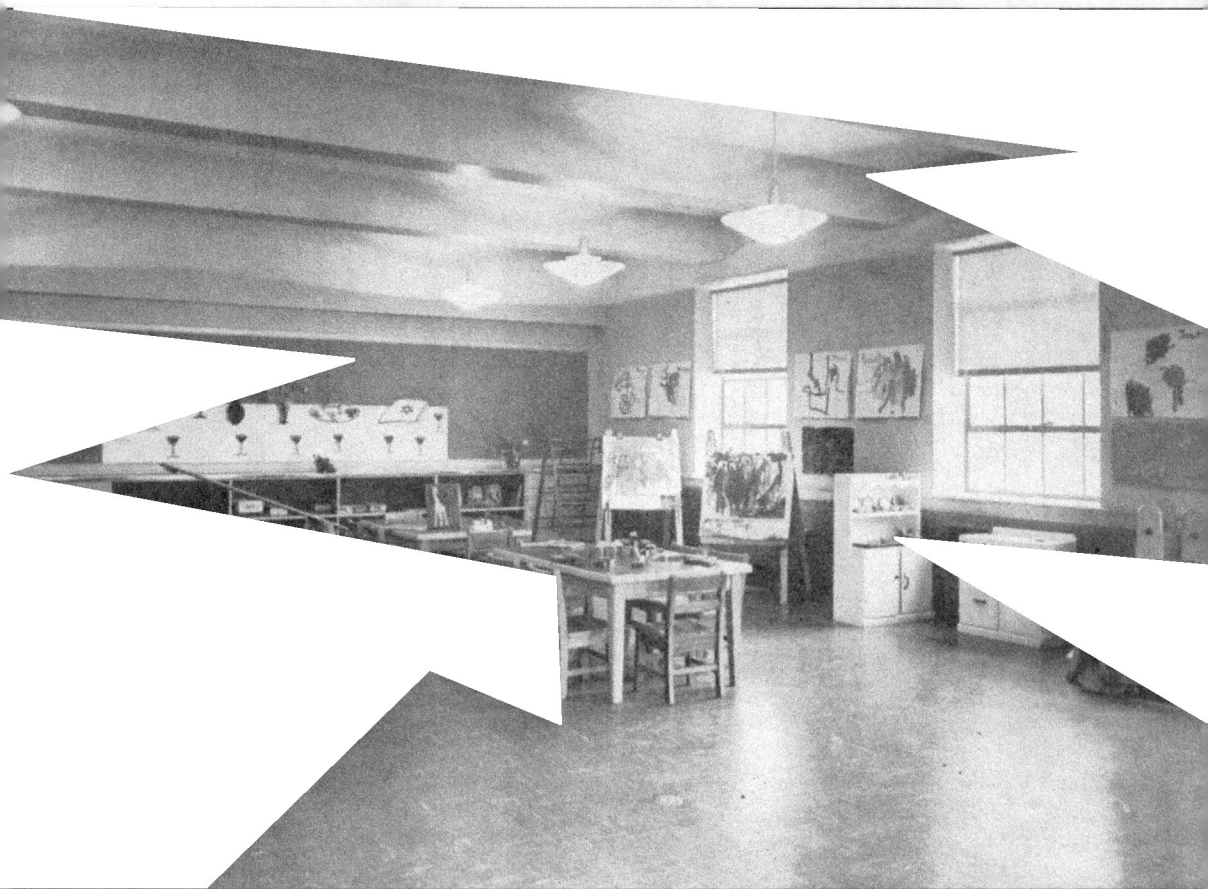

In the 1950s, Congregation Beth Sholom served as the only Orthodox-led Hebrew school for a Jewish population, most of whom sent their children to public schools. (Courtesy of Congregation Beth Sholom.)

'He who denies a child religious knowledge robs him of his inheritance."
—Sanhedrin, 91 B.

The Beth Sholom Hebrew School maintained classes for children of the congregation and greater community at large who attended public school. Note the one-piece desk with the tablet arm for book placement. On the front wall to the right of the room is a chart containing the letters of the Aleph-Beit. Toward the ceiling are the same letters in a row with the cursive Hebrew letters underneath. (Courtesy of Congregation Beth Sholom.)

Rabbi Klaperman led an illustrious life replete with accomplishments. In addition to his work in the rabbinate, he practiced law, was a professor of law at Hofstra University School of Law, and was a professor of religion at the University of Iowa and Yeshiva University. He has also authored a number of books, including, with his late wife, Libby, a four-volume history of the Jews and the history of Yeshiva University. In addition to his local community service, Rabbi Klaperman was very active in Jewish affairs worldwide, including his leadership role with the New York Conference on Soviet Jewry in 1956, and on various organizations, such as the Rabbinical Council of America, the Rabbinic Alumni, the College Alumni of Yeshiva University, and the National Rabbinic ORT Committee. He also was a chaplain in the Canadian army in World War II. As the founder of Hillel, which later merged with the Hebrew Institute of Long Island to become the Hebrew Academy of Five Towns and Rockaways (HAFTR), he was honored at a dinner in 2012 celebrating his 91st birthday. (Courtesy of Reuben Maron and HAFTR.)

The Young Israel of Woodmere began in the private home of Myron and Beverly Beinenfeld in the summer of 1955. Rabbi Benjamin Kamenetzky served as the founding rabbi of the congregation, which was originally called the Eitz Chaim Jewish Center. After only a few months, it relocated to the building that the Yeshiva of South Shore had just started, on 4 Oak Street in Woodmere. It then relocated to a home on the corner of Forest Avenue and Peninsula Boulevard. It finally found a permanent home at 859 Peninsula Boulevard (above), where it serves as one of the largest Young Israel–affiliated synagogues in America.

The synagogue was renovated in 1987 to accommodate the large number of families. It currently has seven daily minyanim for *shacharis* (morning prayers), including a *vasikin* (sunrise) minyan; seven Shabbos minyanim; including a young couples' minyan; nusach sfard minyan; and teen minyan. There are multiple weekday mincha-maariv minyanim, daily shiurim for men and women, daf yomi multiple times a day, and many more religious amenities and programs, including a lending library and social hall.

Thursday, June 21, 1956

Etz Chaim, New Temple, Holds Third Service

Rabbi Benj. Kamentzky

A new Jewish congregation, Etz Chaim, will hold its third service this Saturday morning under the direction of Rabbi Benjamin Kamenetsky. The temporary temple is a store at 732 West Broadway, Woodmere.

Etz Chaim, an orthodox congregation, is composed at present of about 40 families. It met, without organization, in the late months of 1955. It became formally organized in Jan. of this year with Samuel Zuckerberg, Manfred Lehman, Myron Bienenfeld, Joseph Herman and Meyer Greenberg among the founders.

Rabbi Kamenetsky, whose father is dean of Torah Vodath in New York, is a graduate of the Rabbinical College of Baltimore. He comes to Woodmere from Congregation Sons of Jacob in Brooklyn.

The new congregation is in the midst of registration for the Hebrew School which it intends opening this year.

The synagogue originated in a storefront on West Broadway in Woodmere and moved a few times until it found a home on the corner of Forest and Peninsula Boulevard, where it remained until a new building was completed at 859 Peninsula Boulevard in Woodmere in 1962. Above is the original structure of the synagogue on the corner of Forest Avenue and Peninsula Boulevard. It has been a residence since the synagogue moved out in the 1960s.

Rabbi Benjamin Kamenetzky served as the founding rabbi of the Young Israel of Woodmere. After being evicted from its home on West Broadway, the shul relocated to Yeshiva of South Shore, which had just opened at 4 Oak Street in Woodmere; at that time, Rabbi Kamenetzky was dean of the yeshiva. Shown here is Rabbi Kamenetzky with Robert Schulman, the first bar mitzvah boy in the fledgling synagogue. Robert has since become Dr. Robert Schulman, a well-known internist affiliated with Maimonides Hospital in Brooklyn.

As the congregation grew, Rabbi Kamenetzky's role in the yeshiva made it too difficult to tend to both the yeshiva and synagogue. In 1960, English-born scholar Rabbi Shaya Sidney Lebor, who had studied in the Mir Yeshiva in Poland until the onset of World War II in 1939, was appointed to lead the young congregation. A true Torah scholar and an erudite speaker, he had served as a rabbi at the Bikur Cholim Sheveth Achim Synagogue in New Haven and in a Brooklyn congregation before coming to Young Israel of Woodmere in 1960. Though Rabbi Kamenetzky ceded his position as the pulpit rabbi of Young Israel of Woodmere in order to focus on his duties at the Yeshiva of South Shore, Rabbis Lebor and Kamenetzky maintained a close relationship throughout the years. Rabbi Kamenetzky led High Holy Day prayer services at Young Israel for many years, and Rabbi Lebor taught at the Yeshiva of South Shore. Here, they are seen dancing together at a Yeshiva of South Shore dinner. (Above, courtesy of Arthur Elfenbein.)

The ground-breaking ceremonies for the Young Israel of Woodmere were indeed a festive occasion with a small but vibrant community coming out in full force. Depicted above is Rabbi Sidney Lebor addressing the audience on a podium bedecked with patriotic red, white, and blue bunting on the property at 859 Peninsula Boulevard. Below is a partial view of the crowd. Note that children have front-row seats. Standing at left is the Rebbitzin Sarah Lebor; she served the community alongside her husband until his retirement in 1980.

A devoted building committee of lawyers, architects, and builders spearheaded the construction of the state-of-the-art building for the congregation of the Young Israel of Woodmere in 1961. The synagogue was renovated in 1987 to accommodate the large number of families who moved in over 25 years. It currently has seven daily minyanim for the *shacharis* morning prayers; seven Shabbos minyanim; daily classes for men and women; daf yomi multiple times a day; and many more religious amenities and programs, including a lending library and social hall. Pictured from left to right are Norman Dachs, David Miller, and Joe Peterseil. The two children are Jonathan Dachs (front) and Mordechai Kamenetzky (rear). (Courtesy of Paul Hanau.)

The interior of the Young Israel was wood-paneled mahogany with velour-covered seats in theater-like pews. The bimah was in the center of the synagogue in the Orthodox tradition. Depicted is Maurice Zalta holding a Torah scroll while the congregation circled with the *lulav* and *esrog* during a Sukkot service. (Courtesy of Arthur Elfenbein.)

The ark of the synagogue (*Aron Kodesh*) had the capacity for more than seven Torah scrolls. Depicted from left to right are Nahum Gordon, Rabbi Dovid Spiegel, Jacob Heller, and Manny Libin at a Torah scroll dedication. (Courtesy of Arthur Elfenbein.)

The addition of a Torah scroll is always a most joyous occasion for any synagogue. Depicted are Phillip "Feivi" Fuchs leading a procession that is escorting a new Torah into the sanctuary. Behind Fuchs are Marvin Weissman (left) and Irwin Luxenberg (clapping). (Courtesy of Arthur Elfenbein.)

Rabbi Lebor poses with all the presidents of the synagogue, from its founding until 1962, when this photograph was taken at a dinner of Yeshiva of South Shore. From left to right are Emanuel "Manny" Libin, Sam Weill, Frank Herman, Joe Peterseil, Rabbi Lebor, Edward Koppel, and Gabriel Deutsch.

Rudy and Ida Rosen moved to the Five Towns in the early 1950s. Originally members of Congregation Sons of Israel, they became members of the Young Israel when they moved across the street from the shul. They threw themselves into every activity of the new congregation. Rudy served on almost every committee that tended to the physical needs of the building and congregation. After his passing, an annual award was established in Rudy's memory for teens involved in communal work. Shown here is Rudy and Ida Rosen's home on Peninsula Boulevard in the mid-1950s. Peninsula Boulevard was a small two-lane road at the time. Their home was open to all community members. (Both, courtesy of Ida Rosen.)

Jacob Heller made a tremendous impact on the life of Young Israel of Woodmere. Always sharply dressed, Heller had a magnificent, resonating baritone voice that could make a room stand still. He also had a beautiful singing voice, and many people fondly remember how he masterfully led the davening on the *Yamim Noraim* (High Holy Day services) for many years at the Young Israel of Woodmere. (Courtesy of Arthur Elfenbein.)

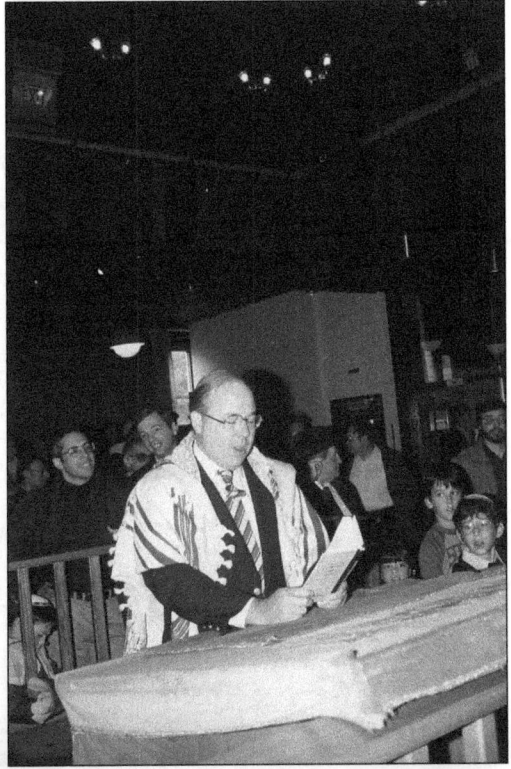

Rabbi Lebor is shown presenting awards to prominent synagogue members, from left to right, Ira Herenstein, Sam Weil, Rabbi Sidney Lebor, Joe Peterseil, and Aaron Jacoby.

Julius (pictured at left) and Grace Rosenszweig moved to Woodmere in 1959 after having resided for nine years in the Parkchester section of the Bronx, where Julius was a vice president of the Young Israel of Parkchester. He was president of Young Israel of Woodmere from 1963 to 1966. He and Grace were honored in 1966. From left to right are Julius Rosenszweig, Congressman Herbert Tenzer, Rabbi Lebor, and Aaron Jacoby. (Courtesy of the Rosenszweig family.)

Seen here are four individuals whose involvement in Young Israel was crucial to its growth. From left to right are Maurice (Moshe) Friedman; Milton Schulman, who served as president of Young Israel in 1960; Adele Goldstein; and Leonard Goldstein, who served as president of Young Israel in 1962. (Courtesy of Arthur Elfenbein.)

Through the years, the Young Israel of Woodmere became a center of philanthropy and Jewish life in the Five Towns. Prominent rabbis and Torah sages often visited it. Depicted here from left to right are Rabbie Reuvain Feinstein (the son of Rabbie Moshe Feinstein), Rabbi Benjamin Kamenetzky, Rabbi Lebor (who, out of deference and respect, gave the sage his place on the synagogue's platform), and Rabbi Moshe Feinstein (at the podium), one of the world's greatest Torah scholars and leading authorities on Jewish law. Below is Emanuel Libin speaking with Rabbi Feinstein. (Below, courtesy of Beverly Libin.)

51

Rabbi Hershel Billet began his tenure as the rabbi of Young Israel of Woodmere in 1981 and continues to serve a congregation that has quadrupled in size since that time to nearly 1,000 families and four rabbis assisting him. Pictured above leading the procession is Jacob Heller, followed by Rabbi Hershel Billet and Norman Bertram. Pictured below, from left to right are David Mandel, executive director of Ohel Children's Home and Family Services; Rabbi Hershel Billet; Rabbi Yaakov Reisman; Rabbi of Agudath Israel, of Lawrence; and Rabbi Kenneth Hain, of Congregation Beth Sholom in Lawrence. (Above, courtesy of Arthur Elfenbein; below, courtesy of The Jewish Star.)

Rabbi Nuchim Zvi Kornmehl *zt"l* arrived in the Five Towns at the invitation of a small group that was forming the Young Israel of Lawrence-Cedarhurst in 1964. Rabbi Kornmehl was then completing a quarter-century as rabbi of Agudas Achim Synagogue in Albany, New York, and considered the move to Long Island to be closer to his family. Rabbi Kornmehl had arrived in the United States from Vienna, after a brief stay in Belgium, in 1939. He had been born in Poland and moved to Vienna at age six, when his father, Rav Mordechai Kornmehl, became one of the three *dayanim* (rabbinic judges) of Vienna. He studied under his father, and at age 19, when his father died suddenly. Rabbi Kornmehl, a Torah prodigy, was granted *smicha* (ordination) that year and ascended to his father's position. He was responsible for the spiritual welfare of five communities in Vienna. In 1934, Rav Kornmehl married the former Rose Klein *a"h*, the sister of noted Torah activists Stephen and Martin Klein. He wrote numerous Torah novella and responsa. (Courtesy of Arthur Federman.)

The Young Israel of Lawrence-Cedarhurst began in 1964 in a home on Columbia Avenue, which served as not only the home of the congregation but also that of the rabbi. It was purchased for $24,000 by a small group of members of Congregation Beth Sholom. One of them, Murray Kotkes, knew Rabbi Kornmehl (Murray's son had married the rabbi's daughter) and suggested that he be chosen as rabbi. (Courtesy of the Long Island Collection at Hofstra University.)

With the growth of the congregation, a larger facility was purchased one block east on Spruce Street, and with Rabbi Kornmehl's passing, Rabbi Moshe Teitelbaum assumed the role of leadership. (Courtesy of the Long Island Collection at Hofstra University.)

Rabbi Kornmehl married Rose Klein, sister of Viennese chocolatier Stephen Klein, who moved to the United States and founded Barton's Chocolates. An expert in kosher supervision, Rabbi Kornmehl wrote numerous responsa on issues of kosher law. He is seen here inspecting a manufacturing plant to ensure that the standards of kosher were the best.

A brilliant Torah scholar whose first language was Yiddish, Rabbi Kornmehl did not shy away from visiting the local schools and interacting with the young American children. Here, he is seen at the far left visiting a fourth grade class at Yeshiva of South Shore. To his right is school president Louis Goldwyn and Rabbi Charles Schindler, principal.

Arthur and Arlene Federman were founding members of the Young Israel of Lawrence-Cedarhurst and were honored at an annual dinner. Seen here, they are receiving a plaque that attests to their pioneering efforts. (Courtesy of Arthur Federman.)

At the 2015 banquet of the Young Israel of Lawrence-Cedarhurst honoring Beth and Nathan Fruchter, the guests of honor pose with their rabbi and local public officials. From left to right are Bruce Blakeman, councilman; Howard Koppel, Nassau County legislator; Nathan Fruchter; Beth Fruchter; Anthony J. Santino, councilman; and Moshe Teitelbaum, rabbi of Young Israel of Lawrence-Cedarhurst.

Rabbi Kornmehl led the congregation until his passing in 1992. During the later years of his life, the congregation chose Rabbi Moshe Teitelbaum as his assistant; he would ultimately succeed Kornmehl. When the congregation expanded, it moved to a new location. Rabbi Kornmehl's legacy lives on in the Five Towns, as his home and *beis midrash* now serve as the site of the Tifereth Zvi Minyan, named in his honor, where his devoted disciple, Rabbi Pinchas Chatzinoff, serves as rabbi.

Rabbi Dovid Spiegel was born in the Bronx. His father, Rabbi Pinchos Eliyahu Spiegel, was the Hasidic rebbe of Ostrov Kalushin. He is shown here (left) with his mother, Rebbitzin Basha Speigel, and twin brother, Avraham Elchanan. His brother passed away tragically in a car accident in December 1973.

Rabbi Dovid Spiegel is a student of illustrious Torah scholars; among them is Rabbi Aaron Kotler, the Rosh Yeshiva of Beth Medrash Govoah, of Lakewood, New Jersey. Pictured from left to right in the foreground are Rabbi Dovid Spiegel; Rabbi Aaron Kotler (holding a volume); and Rabbi Simcha Soleveitchik of Monsey, New York. Rabbi David Hollander is in the background.

The first Hasidic rebbe to move to the Five Towns, Rabbi Spiegel came with his wife, Devorah (née Leifer), the daughter of the Pittsburgh rebbe. Here, Rabbi Spiegel is shown with his wife and 8 of his 10 daughters in front of their Cedarhurst home. Two more daughters and two sons were born later. (Courtesy of Arthur Elfenbein.)

Many community members crammed the small *shteeble* (Yiddish for a house synagogue) to join in ceremony introducing the first Torah scrolls to the new congregation, which was named simply Congregation Beis Medrash (House of Study). From left to right are Rabbi David Spiegel, George Blumenthal, Ben Topol, Bernard Drucker, obscured, and Rabbi Benjamin Kamenetzky. (Courtesy of R. Dean Blumenthal.)

The original house on West Broadway, which was sold to Rabbi Spiegel by Judge Joel Gewanter, served as both the home of the congregation and the rabbi. There was always a weekly hot kiddush and cholent prepared by Rebbitzin Spiegel. As the rebbe became a mentor and guide to scores of families, the small home could no longer maintain the growth of the synagogue. In 2010, a new building was constructed adjacent to the original home. (Above, courtesy of the Long Island Collection at Hofstra University.)

Congregation Derech Emunah was built in 1905, with a seating capacity for 600 persons, "at the corner of Ocean and Vernam Avenues" (199 Beach Sixty-seventh Street) in Arverne. It was one of the city's largest congregations. Originally a mixed-seating synagogue, where "the wearing of the hat was not compulsory," it quickly developed into an Orthodox synagogue. After 97 years, it was gutted, almost certainly by an arsonist, in 2002. It was reduced to conducting services in a run-down double-wide trailer on the Rockaway Peninsula in Queens. A developer bought the property and ordered the Orthodox synagogue to vacate the trailer right after Yom Kippur 2009 to make way for the bulldozers and backhoes. This was the plight of many synagogues in the western end of the Rockaways, whose communities deteriorated and gentrified, without an infusion of young committed Jews. (Courtesy of the Leiman Collection.)

Rabbi Eugene Cohen led the congregation during its prime years. From left to right are Rabbi Eugene Cohen; Dr. Samuel Belkin, president of Yeshiva University; and Nathan Boriskin, the president of the Popular Priced Dress Manufacturers Group, an organization of dress manufacturers with more than 350 members.

Rabbi Shalom Rivkin was an illustrious scholar who served as rabbi at the Young Israel of Wavecrest-Bayswater. In 1970, he was appointed as rabbi of the Young Israel of Wavecrest-Bayswater. He served then as the chief *dayan* (judge) of the Beth Din (Court of Jewish Law) of America Rabbinical Council of America, a post he held for 15 years. He was a renowned expert in all matters of Jewish law and an international authority on Jewish divorce law, travelling as far as Russia to help facilitate them according to Jewish tradition. At right, he is seen affixing a mezuzah on a doorpost on the Bikur Cholim Synagogue in Seattle, where he first served as a rabbi in 1959. Below, he is inspecting a Torah scroll at the Young Israel of Wavecrest-Bayswater. He was appointed chief rabbi of St. Louis, Missouri, in 1983, the city in which he had once held a pulpit in 1949. He served until 2005 and passed away in 2011. (Courtesy of Baruch C. Cohen, Esq.)

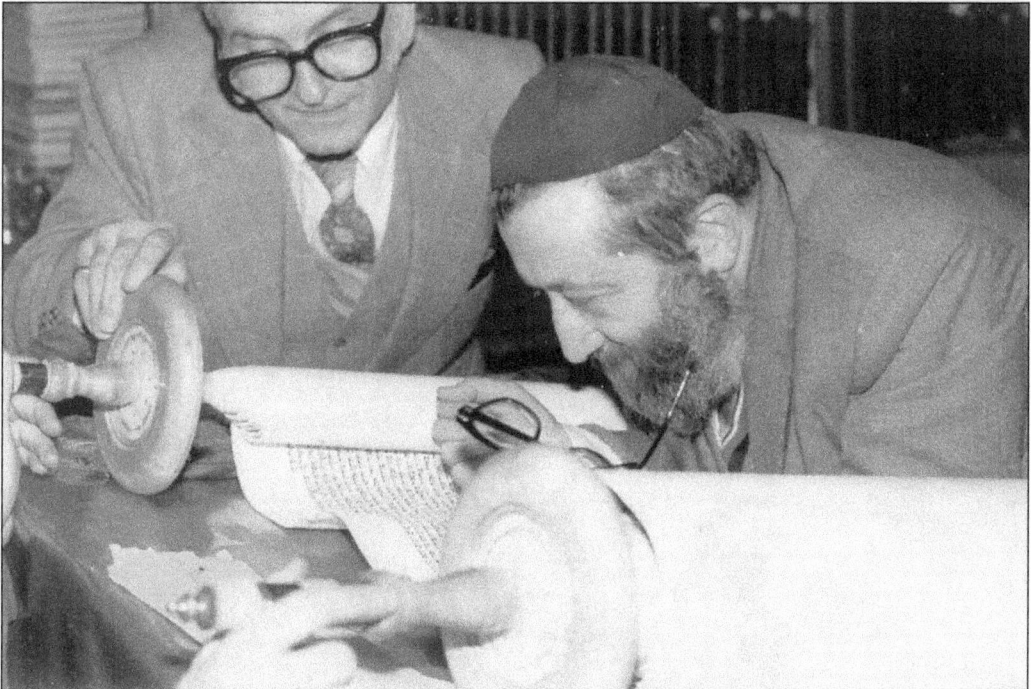

Rabbi Moshe Chait followed Rabbi Rivkin as rabbi of Young Israel of Wavecrest-Bayswater. Rav Chait was a student of Rav Dovid Leibowitz at Yeshiva Chofetz Chaim in Williamsburg, Brooklyn, and a teacher at Yeshiva University. He moved to Israel in 1970 to begin the Jerusalem branch of Yeshiva Chofetz Chaim. Pictured above from left to right are Rabbi Moshe Chait, Rabbi Benjamin Kamenetzky, and Rabbi Yochanan Chait, who remained friends since the time they met at Yeshiva Chofetz Chaim in 1942. Pictured below is Rabbi Chait in his position as the rabbi of Young Israel of Bayswater.

Congregation Ohr Torah served as the first Orthodox congregation in North Woodmere, Long Island. It was founded and led by Rabbi Theodore (Meshulem) Jungreis, who, together with his esteemed wife, Esther, led the congregation for close to 30 years. They were known for their creativity in bringing Jews closer to the Jewish faith and practice. Rabbi Jungreis was born to a long line of rabbinical leaders. His father was the rabbi of his native Gyöngyös, Hungary. Rabbi Theodore Jungreis was ordained at the young age of 18. When the Germans invaded, he was held at Bergen-Belsen concentration camp until the liberation. The Rebitzin Esther, as she is known world over, founded the dynamic Hineini (Heritage Center) in November 1973 to help Jews find their way back to Jewish belief and practice.

Rabbi Jungreis is carrying a Sefer Torah, which was donated by one of his congregants. (Courtesy of Arthur Elfenbein.)

The Five Towns rabbis had a wonderful rapport with each other, often making impromptu meetings at functions that brought representatives of the growing communities together. Here, Rabbi Jungreis (left) talks with Rabbi Sydney Lebor of Young Israel of Woodmere (right) in the parking lot of the local Waldbaum supermarket on Peninsula Boulevard. (Courtesy of Arthur Elfenbein.)

In the fall of 1954, 50 houses were completed as the antecedent of 2,000 homes planned as the North Woodmere community. By June 1955, a group of Jewish residents, led by Herb Shumer, established a house of worship in an unused garage in the rear of Hoeffner's Gulf Station on Rosedale Road. Herb Shumer was the temple's first president. The name Valley Stream South Jewish Center was eventually changed to Temple Hillel. Ground-breaking ceremonies were held on July 22, 1956, at Temple Hillel's current location at 1000 Rosedale Road in North Woodmere. The new building was ready for the High Holy Days of 1956. (Courtesy of longislandexchange.com.)

Rabbi Morris Friedman was installed as spiritual leader of Temple Hillel on Selichot Night, September 14, 1963. He and his wife, Adi, served the congregation for 30 years in an extremely graceful and generous manner. His involvement with the community at large and his embracing of the fledgling Orthodox community in the Five Towns earned him respect and admiration of many of his peers and community members from across the area. He encouraged the growth of yeshivas and even advised some of his own congregants to move to the Five Towns and that they help develop the yeshivas and Orthodox shuls. Pictured above, from left to right are Rabbi Benjamin Kamenetzky, Stuart Rafkind, and Rabbi Morris Friedman. Below, Rabbi Morris Friedman, Rabbi Theodore Jungreis, and Rabbi Benjamin Kamenetzky are celebrating communal events together with members of their respective synagogues.

On October 26, 1984, Pres. Ronald Reagan visited and spoke at Temple Hillel. It was the first time since Pres. George Washington visited the Touro Synagogue in Newport, Rhode Island, that an American synagogue received a US president. This was arranged through the good graces of US senator Alfonse D'Amato, a longtime friend of Rabbi Friedman. Upon completion of a program in the main sanctuary, Rabbi and Mrs. Friedman hosted a luncheon at their home. President Reagan enjoyed the rebbitzen's cooking. Above, Rabbi and Mrs. Friedman (far left) are standing with their family members and President Reagan. Below, Rabbi Friedman is discussing an issue with Senator D'Amato. (Above, courtesy of the Friedman family.)

The Sisterhood of Temple Beth El

invites you to hear our
distinguished rabbi

DR. EDWARD T. SANDROW

who will discuss
The Platforms of the Political Parties:
Do they relate to the
social problems of our times?

Monday Sept. 9, 1968

Champagne Reception   12:00 - 12:30
Luncheon   12:30 - 1:15
Register for Education Program
Baby Sitter in Attendance

Rabbi Edward Sandrow served the congregation from 1937 until 1971, taking a hiatus to serve as a chaplain in World War II. He served as the chairman of the board of education at the Brandeis School and on various boards of Jewish organizations, including the Jewish Telegraphic Agency and the Board of Directors of the Hebrew University.

Temple Beth El of Cedarhurst, one of the oldest Jewish congregations in the Five Towns, was formed as a Conservative congregation in 1922. It had notable rabbis who served in larger capacities outside the synagogue. The temple also had a Hebrew school. Today, the congregation is much smaller, and the former Hebrew school facilities are rented to the Shulamith School for Girls, an Orthodox school.

Rabbi Irving Miller (standing far left) was born in Kaunas, Lithuania, and first served as the rabbi of Shaaray Tefila before he was appointed as rabbi of Sons of Israel, a synagogue founded in 1928 and chartered to pray in the tradition of Orthodox Judaism. It held to the Orthodox liturgy but configured the sanctuary to allow for mixed seating in the path of Conservative Judaism. Rabbi Miller served as rabbi from 1946 to 1963. The photograph was taken at the dedication of a Torah scroll to Yeshiva of South Shore by Sons of Israel members Elie and Lillian Gut. The Torah was commissioned in honor of their son Ralph's bar mitzvah in 1954, but the passing of the scribe delayed its completion until 1956. The Guts decided to give the Torah to the fledgling Yeshiva of South Shore that had just opened in Woodmere. Mr. Gut is seen carrying the Torah into the building on the cover of this book. From left to right are Rabbi Jacob Kamenecki, dean of Mesivta Torah Vodaath, and father of Rabbi Benjamin Kamenetzky, Dean, Yeshiva of South Shore, who is standing next to him; Rabbi David Hollander, of Mount Eden Jewish Center and president of the Rabbinical Council of America; and Rabbi Irving Miller, of Congregation Sons of Israel. Sitting is the donor Eli Gut.

Lazar Wax served as the cantor for Congregation Sons of Israel for 38 years. A native of Sieu, Romania, Lazar was taken to Auschwitz during World War II where he survived. Cantor Wax z"l served the congregation for 38 years as Chazzan, Torah reader, bar/bat mitzvah instructor, counselor, and friend before retiring to Florida; He returned each High Holiday season for another dozen years thereafter to lead the parallel services. During their decades of devotion to Congregation Sons of Israel, he and his wife, Ida, touched countless lives in the community and beyond. He passed away in December of 2013. From left to right are unidentified, Cantor Wax, Sam Levinson, unidentified, and Rabbi Ralph Pelcowitz.

Cantor David Abikzer served the Sephardic Temple in Cedarhurst. Born in Morocco in 1939, he began his music education in Casablanca, moved to Israel, came to the United States, and graduated from the US School of Music.

The story of Temple Israel is indicative of the changing face of Judaism in the Five Towns. It was founded in 1908 as Temple Israel of Far Rockaway with services held in rented quarters. A white Colonial-style temple was then built at the corner of Roanoke and State Streets in Far Rockaway; this building was later sold to the Orthodox congregation Knesseth Israel. The present building was dedicated in 1930, and it was then that it became Temple Israel of Lawrence. Designed by award-winning architect S. Brian Baylinson, the sanctuary for Temple Israel is acknowledged architecturally as one of the most distinguished and elegant worship centers in the United States highlighted in a publication on synagogue architecture, titled *Synagogues of New York City*. The Hebrew school is now defunct, as the population has become more observant and serves as a preschool for the Jewish Community Center (JCC) of the Five Towns. With dwindling membership and lack of interest in a reform temple in the Five Towns communities, in an interesting repeat of its original fate, plans are being formulate to sell the entire facility to either the Jewish Community Center or an Orthodox organization.

The Sephardic Temple was an architectural masterpiece built in the early 1960s to serve the needs of the Sephardic community of Long Island. It attempted to conserve the Sephardic traditions of prayer, yet adapted the newfound moderations of the Conservative movement in allowing a section with mixed seating—one of the first Sephardic congregations to do so. For their rabbi, they chose Arnold Marans, who had served for eight years prior as rabbi of Congregation United Sephardim of Brooklyn. Rabbi Marans, a graduate of the Jewish Theological Seminary in New York, began his tenure at Sephardic Temple in 1963 and still holds the position of rabbi. He is currently the longest serving pulpit rabbi on Long Island.

Three

DAY SCHOOLS AND YESHIVAS

Residences in South Street, Far Rockaway, N. Y.

In 1937, a coeducational Jewish day school was founded by a group led by Joseph Yurkowitz, with the simple name "Yeshiva of the Rockaways." It was located in the balcony section of Congregation Anshei Sfard in Arverne, New York. Rabbi Mordechai Shuchatowitz, rabbi of Congregation Shaarey Zedek in Edgemere, served as principal. In 1946, Dr. Irving Agus served for one year. Rabbi Harold I. Leiman then took over and developed and grew the school, serving as principal and dean until 1960. He returned in 1971 and helped the merger with Hillel Country Day School. In 1939, the school moved to Far Rockaway, to a large complex on Beach Nineteenth Street that had originally served ill mothers located across the street from the Genadeen Hotel. With the move, the school changed its name to the Hebrew Institute of Long Island. (Courtesy of the Leiman Collection.)

The high school division of HILI (as it was called) opened on the top floor of Congregation Shaaray Tefila in 1951 and eventually joined the elementary division in what was called the E Building on Seagirt Boulevard. In 1978, as the population looking for a coeducational school shifted toward the Five Towns, HILI merged with the Hillel School in Lawrence to form the Hebrew Academy of the Five Towns and Rockaway (popularly known by its initials as HAFTR). (Courtesy of R. Dean Blumenthal.)

HIGH SCHOOL

HEBREW

RABBI ZEV ALTUSKY

RABBI MEIR BRAYER

RABBI AVRAM COHEN

RABBI ISAAC DAVIS   RABBI OVADIAH DUBIN   RABBI REUVEN FEINSTEIN

Hebrew high school staff HILI included well-known Talmudic scholars. Among staff were Rabbi Zev Altusky, a brilliant Talmudist whose son now serves as the Rosh Yeshiva of Yeshiva Darchei Torah; Rabbi Ovadiah Dubin, an expert in *tanach*; and Rabbi Reuven Feinstein, the son of Rabbi Moses Feinstein. (Courtesy of R. Dean Blumenthal.)

As the only day school in the area, the student body of the Hebrew Institute of Long Island was varied. It was comprised of a diverse population. Some of the students came from homes that were not Sabbath observant, while others came from prestigious rabbinic families, among them the grandson of the Ponovezer Rav, Rabbi Kahanamen; the children of noted rabbis, such as Rabbi Pelcovitz, of the Congregation Knesseth Israel; Rabbi Mordechai Berkowitz, who was the rabbi of the HILI shul; and the children of Rabbi Chavel, the rabbi of Edgemere and the editor and annotator of the very popular *Mosad HaRav Kook* edition of the *Ramban al HaTorah* (Nachmanides in the Bible). The HILI kindergarten and third grades are pictured in 1959. (Both, courtesy of R. Dean Blumenthal.)

HEBREW INSTITUTE
OF
LONG ISLAND
1957-58
4-2

Pictured above are students in the 1957 fourth grade class. The students of HILI prided themselves in the large campus that had four buildings. Over the years, the campus changed hands to institutions of Jewish interest. HILI sold the buildings to the Hartman Young Men's Hebrew Association (YMHA), which then rented the facilities to Yeshiva Darchei Torah, which eventually bought them and developed the property into a massive campus with many buildings educating nearly 1,800 students. (Both, courtesy of R. Dean Blumenthal.)

A TOUR OF THE WHITE HOUSES

The school comes into view. The bell is ringing; students dash to their classes –

Welcome to HILI!

The day begins with morning Hebrew classes . . .

HILI's basketball coach Bill Wiener was a major contributor in the growth and development of what today is a 22-team yeshiva high school basketball league in the New York–New Jersey area. Coach Wiener began as a volunteer at the Hebrew Institute of Long Island in 1959 and coached there until 1983. He returned to the sidelines in 1995 at the Rambam Mesivta High School until his passing at the age of 85. Under Wiener's leadership, HILI quickly became a powerhouse in the then Jewish Basketball League. His teams compiled a 345-155 record and won 13 championships. His players were taught to play hard and with passion and love for the game and with respect for your teammates and opponents. Most importantly, he stressed always conducting oneself as a Torah-loving Jew. His coaching success was a direct result of the combination of basketball knowledge and the ability to motivate and influence young men in all facets of life. Pictured below, HILI player R. Dean Blumenthal takes a shot. (Courtesy of Avrum Stein and the Blumenthal family.)

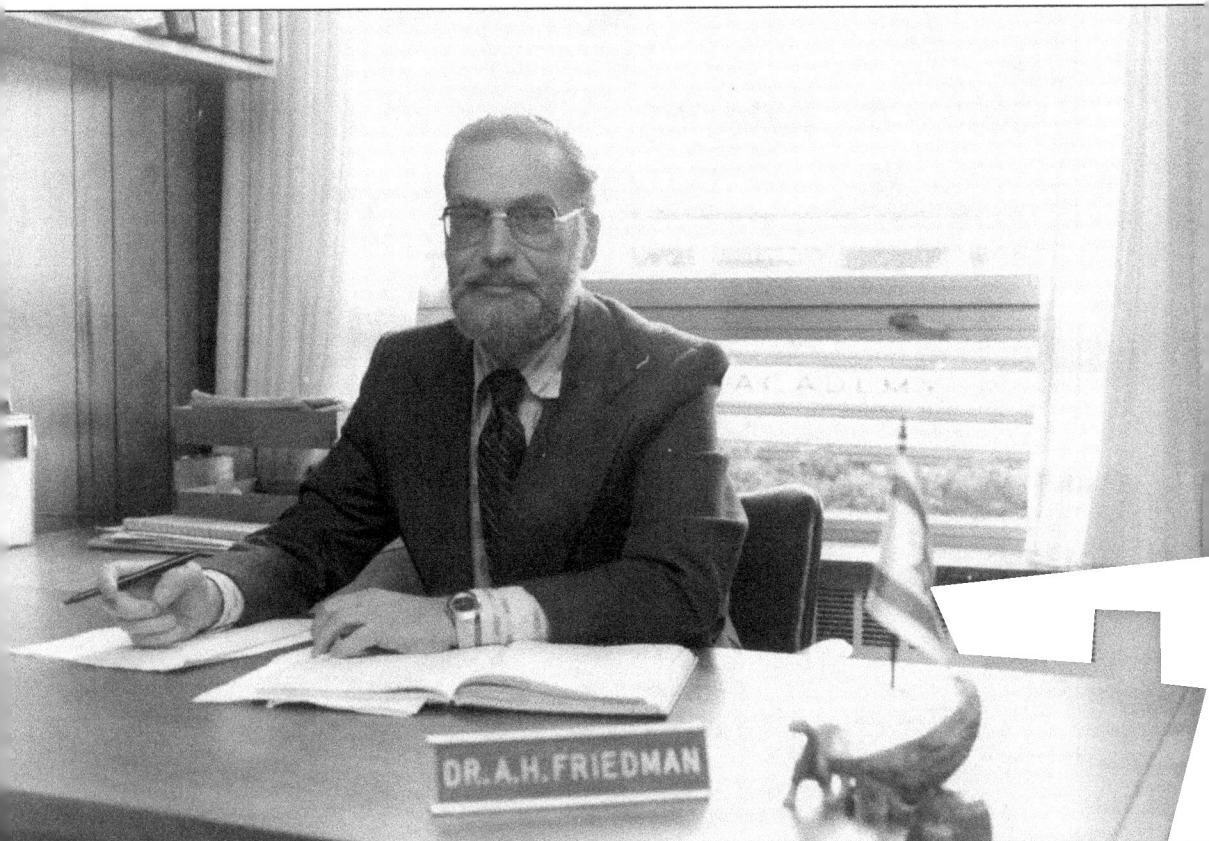

Dr. Armin H. Friedman was the founding principal of the Hebrew Academy of Long Beach (HALB) Yeshivat Lev in 1954. Rabbi Friedman was born in Europe and could recall when the transport of Jews from the Lodz ghetto arrived at Auschwitz. At first, HALB primarily served the communities of Oceanside and Long Beach, but soon enough, its influence was felt as one of the primary educational institutions for residents of the Five Towns and Rockaways. Over time, HALB expanded to include a preschool, Lev Chana, and two high schools, Stella K. Abraham High School for Girls and the Davis Renov Stahler High School for Boys located in the Five Towns. Most recently, HALB purchased the Number No. 6 Public School, where it will move the Long Beach campus. (Courtesy of Richard Hagler and the Hebrew Academy of Long Beach.)

Hebrew Academy of Long Beach

ב״ה

May 7, 1954

OFFICERS

President
Dr. O. S. Glatt
Vice-President
Edward Diamond
Treasurer
Robert Gleicher
Financial Secretary
Jack Shaw
Secretary
Stanley Amsel
458 W. Market St., Long Beach
Telephone — LO 6-3974

BOARD OF EDUCATION

Mrs. Belle Glatt
Mrs. Nettie Mindel
Edward Diamond
Rabbi Ephraim Kolatch
Morton Kronenberg
Cyrus O. Levenson

SPONSORS

Abraham Alpert
Stanley Amsel
Rabbi Saul Baily
Cantor Abraham Brun
Cantor Aaron Caplow
Edward Diamond
Al Eagle
Rabbi A. Eiler
Dr. O. S. Glatt
Robert Gleicher
Rabbi Solomon Goldfarb
Nathan Goldstein
Dr. Louis Gottlieb
Howard Harrison
Rabbi Samuel Horowitz
Isidor Klein
Rabbi Ephraim Kolatch
A. Krieger
Morton Kronenberg
Philip Lewis
Hillel Meyers
Dr. Nisan Mindel
Rabbi Amos Miller
Jack Nathan
A. Newborn
Leon Ohl
Julius Quittman
Jack Shaw
Siegfried Sonnenberg
Mendel Turitz
David Wachstock

LADIES AUXILIARY

Chairman
Pearl Kronenberg
Regina Adler
Sunny Alpert
Bernice Amsel
Hannah Brun
Mildred Eagle
Rose Feinroth
Belle Glatt
Beatrice Gleicher
Sophia Goldfarb
Mollie Kolatch
Vita Meyers
Nettie Mindel
Barbara Shapiro
Helen Turitz

Dear Friend:

One of the most phenomenal developments in recent American Jewish history has been the rapid growth of the Hebrew Day School movement throughout the country. North and South, East and West, American Jewry is beginning to realize the advantages of and the need for an intensive program of Jewish education for our children.

The Jewish community of Long Beach with the cooperation of Torah Umesorah, National Society for Hebrew Day Schools, has taken steps toward the establishment of such a school in our midst, the Hebrew Academy of Long Beach. We would like you to become acquainted with the scope of our goals, the nature of our work, and our relation to your Jewish community.

You are cordially invited, therefore, to attend an Open Meeting of the Hebrew Academy of Long Beach to be held at the

HOTEL RICHMOND
351 West Broadway   Long Beach, New York
on
Sunday, May 16th, 1954 at 8:30 p.m.

A rich and varied program has been prepared. Our guest speaker will be

DR. LEO JUNG
Rabbi of The Jewish Center, New York City,
famous author, lecturer and spiritual leader.

THERE WILL BE NO SOLICITATION OF FUNDS.

Refreshments will be served. Come and bring your friends. You will be participating in an historic occasion for the Jewish community of Long Beach.

Sincerely yours,

Dr. O. S. Glatt
President, Hebrew Academy

עשה למען תינוקות של בית רבן

This letter is an appeal for support for the establishment of the Hebrew Academy of Long Beach signed by the first president of the academy, Dr. O.S. Glatt. The Hebrew Academy of Long Beach was the first Hebrew day school in Nassau County and was founded with the help of the national director of the Society for Hebrew Day Schools, Dr. Joseph Kaminetsky. In what can only be divine providence, the four branches of the Hebrew Academy of Long Beach are headed by a grandson of Dr. Joseph Kaminetsky, Rabbi Yisroel Kaminetsky, who was appointed *rosh yeshiva* (dean) in 2014. (Courtesy of Richard Hagler and the Hebrew Academy of Long Beach.)

Capt. Hyman Friedman, one of the
initial donors to the Hebrew Academy
of Long Beach, served as an officer
in the US Army during World War I.
His magnanimous gift to the fledgling
institution helped create the enormous
Torah educational institute it is today.
(Courtesy of Richard Hagler and the
Hebrew Academy of Long Beach.)

This photograph depicts a scroll of honor being presented to Ari Goldberg, a supporter of the
Hebrew Academy, in recognition of his contributions toward the fledging academy. Pictured from
left to right are Irving Landau, Charles Avnet, Nassau County executive Eugene Nickerson, Ari
Goldberg, Marvin Beinenfeld, Congressman Herbert Tenzer, and Menashe "Nash" Kestenbaum.
(Courtesy of Richard Hagler and the Hebrew Academy of Long Beach.)

Numerous dignitaries attended the ground breaking of the first building of the Hebrew Academy of Long Beach. Among those pictured are New York state assemblyman Jerry Kremer (sitting center), Nassau County executive Eugene Nickerson (to Kremer's left), and Congressman Herbert Tenzer (sitting at far right). (Courtesy of Richard Hagler and the Hebrew Academy of Long Beach.)

Philanthropist Morris Morgenstern, who was involved in almost every Jewish cause in Nassau County, is seen putting a shovel to the ground at the ground-breaking ceremonies for the Hebrew Academy. The sign behind him reads, "We are building our new Hebrew Academy of Long Beach for Torah, for our children, for our parents and our Country." (Courtesy of Richard Hagler and the Hebrew Academy of Long Beach.)

Congressman Herbert Tenzer is handing a flag that flew over the US Capitol in Washington to an honor student at the Hebrew Academy of Long Beach. (Courtesy of Richard Hagler and the Hebrew Academy of Long Beach.)

Republican Assembly majority leader Joseph Carlino presents a gift of a check to the executive staff and the members of the Board of Directors of the Hebrew Academy of Long Beach. From left to right are two unidentified men, Assemblyman Joseph Carlino, and Dr. Armin H. Friedman. (Courtesy of Richard Hagler and the Hebrew Academy of Long Beach.)

Unlike the HILI, HALB was not a coeducational institution, and although the boys and girls studied in the same building, they were separated for their classes. The first-grade boys' class of 1965 is depicted here. (Courtesy of Richard Hagler and the Hebrew Academy of Long Beach.)

Rabbi Isser Yehuda Unterman (1886–1976), the Ashkenazi chief rabbi of Israel from 1964 until 1972, is pictured on a visit to the Hebrew Academy of Long Beach in 1964. He is seated in the center (third from left and right) surrounded by unidentified rabbis and dignitaries. (Courtesy of Richard Hagler and the Hebrew Academy of Long Beach.)

Rabbi Joseph Ber Soloveitchik was a most prominent Talmudist and a foremost thinker, philosopher, leader, and Talmudic scholar. He was the rosh yeshiva of the Rabbi Isaac Elchanan Theological Seminary. He is depicted here testing and discussing Talmudic concepts with the most senior class at the Hebrew Academy of Long Beach. Rabbi Friedman, a student of Rabbi Soleveitchik, is seen standing to his left. (Both, courtesy of Richard Hagler and the Hebrew Academy of Long Beach.)

The Whiton Estate was built by Henry Devereux Whiton, a corporate executive and philanthropist in the 1800s, and was bought by the Lawrence Country Day School in 1920. In 1993, it was purchased by the HALB to be used as a girls' high school. The purchase prompted the village of Hewlett Bay Park to ban the use of the school building as a synagogue and to restrict the number of students who could pray together there at any given time to 75. After a successful lawsuit, the Village dropped the restrictions, and the school is now a thriving center for Jewish education.

A Dr. Levine, from East New York, was a righteous Jew whose children left the fold and moved to Woodmere. They changed their name to Lee and purchased a sprawling estate on a lake. When Dr. Levine would stay in Woodmere, he would walk from his children's sprawling estate to come to help make a minyan in Cedarhurst. After the passing of Lee family members, the Lee Estate was neglected and stood for many years in disrepair. It was finally purchased and developed into the HALB's Davis Renov Stahler High School (DRS) Yeshiva High School for boys.

Yeshiva of South Shore began on 4 Oak Street in Woodmere in a home that was bequeathed by Hyman and Rebecca Feuerstein for the sole purpose of the furtherance of Jewish education. Though Hyman and his wife, Rebecca, were members in Congregation Sons of Israel, and not Orthodox, they were interested in Jewish education. After his passing, the family was reluctant to donate the house, and it was left in disrepair for many months until it was finally given to the yeshiva. After much work, the Yeshiva of South Shore opened in September 1956. Rabbi Benjamin Kamenetzky is pictured at right in front of the bequeathed Feuerstein Memorial Hall.

Dr. Joe Kaminetsky had been a counselor back in the 1920s at Camp Mohegan, probably the first Orthodox sleepaway camp in America. He had two campers, Lester and Bernie Feuerstein, whose father, Hyman, had wanted the boys to remain traditional Jews and was very interested in Jewish continuity. Dr. Kaminetsky was able to influence Bernie and Lester who had changed his name to Forrest to allow the building to be given to the yeshiva. In this photograph, the president of Yeshiva of South Shore, Moshe Katz, is presenting resolutions of gratitude to Lester and Bernard Feuerstein for allowing the donation of their father's home to serve as the first building of Yeshiva of South Shore.

Rabbi Benjamin Kamenetzky and Moshe Katz are accepting the charter establishing Yeshiva of South Shore as part of the Torah U'Mesorah network of Jewish day schools and yeshivas. They are shown here together with Samuel C. Feuerstein, president of Torah Umesorah, the National Society for Hebrew Day Schools.

Rabbi Aaron Kotler was the chairman of the Rabbinical Advisory Council of Torah Umesorah, the National Society for Hebrew Day Schools. Here, he is seen together with Samuel C. Feuerstein, president of Torah Umesorah, as he presented Moshe Katz, president of Yeshiva of South Shore, with the charter to officially accept as a member school.

Pictured with Rabbi Benjamin Kamenetzky and Rabbi Abraham Shimano is a kindergarten class in the Oak Street building.

These students are praying in the small sanctuary in the new school on Oak Street. The covering of the ark was a quilted tapestry with the names of the 12 tribes of Israel sewn by the students of the girls' division of the new yeshiva.

Preparing for Passover in April 1957, the young boys are practicing the holiday rituals together with their rebbe with a model seder, complete with matzoh and grape juice that took place in the main hall of the yeshiva.

The first grade class is posing for a picture together with their teacher, Rabbi Baruch Glatzer. Students are, from top step down, left to right, Owen Bergman, Ronnie Lipstein, Sheldon Lieb, Evan Lipschutz, Sandy Klein, Avi Samuels, Joseph Fox, Chaim Katz, Stuart Wax, Baruch Klein, Gerald Bamberger, Avi Weinberg, Fred Schulman, Mutty Kamenetzky, and Yaakov Thaler.

In 1957, the yeshiva purchased another home one block away on Pine Street to be used as the girls' school. That school lasted until 1963, when it divested from Yeshiva of South Shore and became known as the Torah Academy for Girls in Far Rockaway.

Among the festive holidays is Purim. Here, the girls' division of Yeshiva of South Shore proudly presents the cast of characters in their *Purim Shpiel*, the traditional play that depicts the story of the Jews in Persia who were saved by Mordechai and Esther from Haman's plot to annihilate them.

Involved in almost every Jewish educational endeavor, philanthropist Morris Morgenstern took an interest in Yeshiva South Shore and pledged to name the girls' school the Sadie B. Morgenstern School for Girls in memory of his beloved wife. He is holding a model of the new building he envisioned with two wings, one for boys and one for girls. The girls' school split off, and the building was never constructed. In the photograph above, Morgenstern is seen with Minna Glick, Sam Harris, Queen County district attorney Ed Silver, and Minna Bunim. Below, Mutty Klien, a student in the boys' division, imagines the yeshiva that was never actually built.

Building Plans

Looking over checks received toward building of Said B. Morgenstern School for Girls of the Yeshiva of South Shore are:

Left to Right (Top) Mr. Moshe Katz, President Yeshiva of South Shore, Mr. Joseph Jaspan, General Chairman, Mr. Harry Brown, Chairman Journal Committee.

(Bottom) Mr. Sam Harris, Chairman Building Fund, Mr. Joel Schneierson Chairman of Board of Yeshiva and Rabbi Benjamin Kamentzky, Dean of the School.

In January 1960, plans began in earnest to build a proper facility. Here is a newspaper photograph with committee members Moshe Katz, Joseph Jaspan, Harry Brown, Sam Harris, Joel Schneirson, and Rabbi Benjamin Kamenetzky reviewing checks received toward the building of the school.

Rabbi Benjamin invited New York governor Nelson P. Rockefeller to the first annual banquet of the Yeshiva of South Shore honoring Morris Morgenstern, to be held at the Waldorf Astoria Hotel in Manhattan. From left to right are Morris Morgenstern; Moshe Katz, president of the yeshiva; Rabbi Kamenetzky; and Governor Rockefeller.

Rabbi Isaac Schmidman founded Yeshiva Toras Chaim in 1927 in East New York. It served the communities of East New York and Brownsville until changing demographics and a rise in crime forced it to close in 1963. It merged with the Yeshiva of South Shore in Woodmere, which was established in 1956 by Rabbi Benjamin Kamenetzky, who had once taught under Rabbi Schmidman at Yeshiva Toras Chaim. Zev Isseroff recalls, "In 1963, when on the holiest day in the Jewish Calendar, Yom Kippur night, I was attending services on a synagogue on Ashford street. A few members from the Yeshiva (Toras Chaim) congregation walked over to our synagogue and asked for some volunteers—they did not have a quorum of ten men for the services. We realized that Jewish life in East New York was rapidly coming to an end." Above is a photograph of the Yeshiva Toras Chaim before its conversion to a public school, and at right is an image of Rabbi Schmidman cutting a challah at a yeshiva dinner.

Rabbi Isaac Schmidman was known as a relentless advocate for Jewish education, allowing any Jewish child to enter his yeshiva regardless of the ability to pay. He was cherished by his students and by his staff. Here is shown above sitting in the center of a group photograph of Yeshiva Toras Chaim staff members in the early 1930s and below with students of Yeshiva Toras Chaim in East New York.

In 1963, with the deterioration of the East
New York section of Brooklyn to crime and
the exodus of its Jewish population to the
suburbs, Yeshiva and Mesivta Toras Chaim
of East New York merged with Yeshiva
of South Shore. Rabbi Schmidman had
known Rabbi Kamenetzky as a teacher in
Yeshiva Toras Chaim of East New York,
which helped make his transition easier.
Here, Rabbi Schmidman (left) and Rabbi
Kamenetzky (right) are at the bar mitzvah
of a student and are dancing in celebration
of the completion of the new building of the
newly merged Yeshiva and Mesivta Toras
Chaim of East New York at South Shore.

On a sunny day in 1961, ground was broken for the new building of Yeshiva of South Shore on 1170 William Street. It was a festive occasion, with noted dignitaries and philanthropists in attendance. Pictured from left to right are Eugene H. Nickerson, who later that year became the first Democrat to serve as Nassau County executive; Hempstead town supervisor Palmer Farrington; Queens district attorney Eddie Silver; and industrialist Nathan Boriskin.

Rabbi Benjamin Kamenetzky, dean of Yeshiva of South Shore, stands in front of the newly erected yeshiva school building in 1964. The edifice was built at the cost of $350,000 and contained 12 classrooms, offices, and a lunchroom that doubled as a sanctuary. Outside the building were two massive limestone tablets representing the two tablets that bore the Ten Commandments.

The Yeshiva of South Shore maintained a proud relationship with its alumni, and in 1967, 12 years after its founding, the Yeshiva hosted a reunion of alumni together with the revered sage and father of Rabbi Benjamin Kamenetzky, Rabbi Yaakov Kamenetzky; Rabbi Isaac Schmidman; and Rabbi Benjamin Kamenetzky.

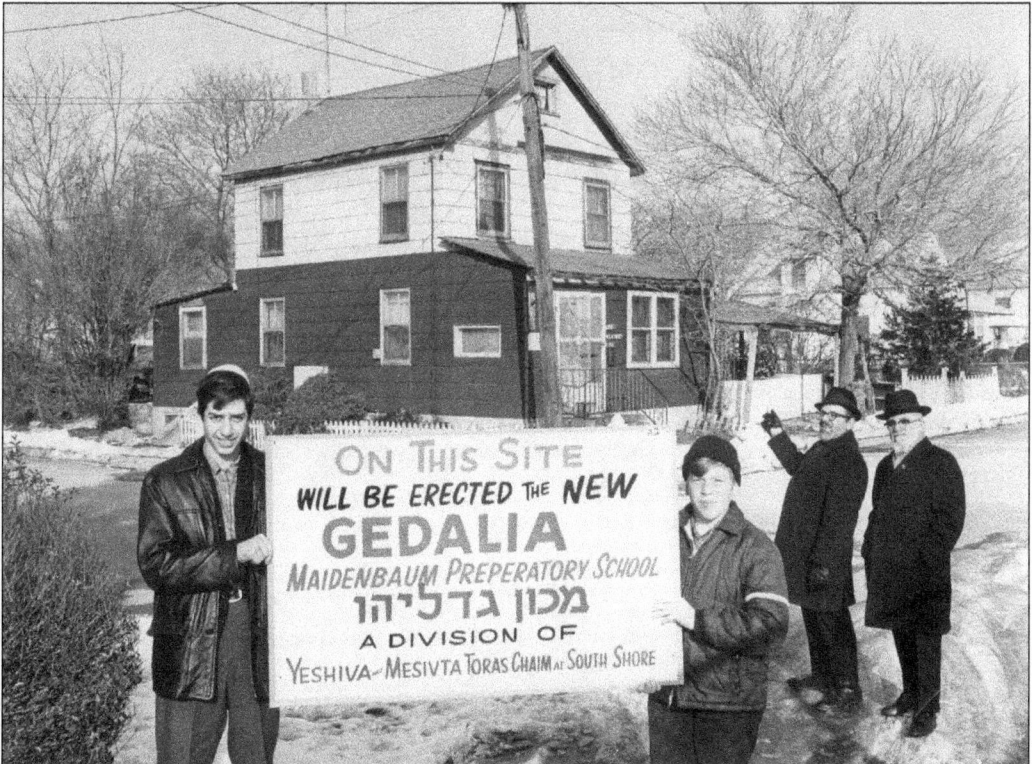

The growth of the yeshiva led to the construction of an additional building in 1970. Esther and Louis Maidenbaum, president of Met Foods, dedicated it in memory of Louis's father, Gedaliah Maidenbaum. The building was to house the middle school of the yeshiva, named Gedaliah Maidenbaum Preparatory School. In the photograph, students Shlomo Leichtung (left) and Ralph Hoffman (right) are standing in front of the site with a sign.

The late 1970s saw an influx of Iranian immigrants who fled their native county because of the rise of Ayatollah Khomeini and the Islamic Revolution. Seen here, Rabbi Yehuda Oelbaum, principal of the Yeshiva of South Shore, greets Elazar Aryeh, who had escaped from Iran with his family and enrolled in Yeshiva of South Shore.

Rabbi Gilbert Klaperman, who wanted to create a coeducational day school with strong commitment to Zionism, established Hillel Country Day School in 1958. In an interview later in life, the rabbi explained that he used to have to drive his children to Yeshiva of Flatbush and wanted a similar type of institution built for them in the local area. HAFTR was established in 1978 as the result of a merger between two schools on the South Shore of Long Island: the Hebrew Institute of Long Island (HILI) in Far Rockaway, Queens, which had served the Rockaway and Five Towns community since 1936; and the Hillel School, which was founded in Lawrence in 1960. The HAFTR High School building is a public school building that was no longer needed because of the shifting population from public to private schools. (Courtesy of HAFTR.)

Rabbi Dr. Zevulun Lieberman served as spiritual leader of Congregation Beth Torah in Brooklyn for half a century. He also was a principal at the Yeshiva of Flatbush High School from 1960 until 1966. Following his career at Yeshiva of Flatbush, Rabbi Lieberman served in the field of Jewish education as the principal of Hillel Country Day School in Lawrence. He died on December 16, 2012, and was buried in Israel next to his son Rabbi Hillel Lieberman, who was brutally murdered by Arab terrorists as he attempted to rescue two burning Sefer Torahs in the Tomb of Joseph in the city of Nablus (Shechem). (Courtesy of Arthur Elfenbein.)

The first kindergarten and first grade classes were held at Congregation Beth Sholom. The school soon blossomed and constructed a building on Washington Avenue, a preschool on Central Avenue, and a junior high school on Frost Lane. (Courtesy of Reuben Maron and HAFTAR.)

Faculty and administration of the Hillel School are pictured in the early 1970s. From left to right are (seated) Barbara Rappaport (math), Marcia Razen (social studies), unidentified, Deborah Robbins (English and Spanish), Judy Levy (secretary); (standing) Arthur Shoum (biology), Rabbi Rappaport (Chumash, Bible), Rabbi Hoffman, Rabbi Israel Chait (Talmud), and Rabbi Chaim Ozer Chait (prophets, Talmud). (Courtesy of Arthur Elfenbein.)

Pictured is a graduating class of Hillel High School. (Courtesy of Arthur Elfenbein.)

The valedictorian is speaking.
(Courtesy of Arthur Elfenbein.)

Dr. Steven Levitz is congratulating Jacob Heller after the prominent attorney delivered the commencement address to the first graduating high school class at Hillel. (Courtesy of Arthur Elfenbein.)

At the dinner for the Hillel School building fund are, from left to right, (seated) Esther Heller, Jacob Heller, Rhoda Miller, Joseph Miller, Evelyn Baron, Charles Baron, and Jesse Aaronson; (standing) Irwin Luxenberg, Joan Luxenberg, Dr. Mel Young, Roberta Young, Arthur Elfenbein, and Celia Aaronson (standing behind her husband). (Courtesy of Arthur Elfenbein.)

The guest of honor, Ben Berkun, is being lifted on a chair by Isaac Sherman of Far Rockaway at the annual dinner of the Hillel Country Day School. (Courtesy of Arthur Elfenbein.)

At a Hillel Country Day School Dinner, some of the major supporters and school activists join in support of the school. From left to right are (seated) two unidentified, Myrna Alpert, and Charles Alpert; (standing) David Kolatch, Esther Kolatch, Alan Weiss, Rochelle Weiss, Herbert Bodek, Ziporrah Bodek, and unidentified. (Courtesy of Arthur Elfenbein.)

Today, the Hebrew Academy of the Five Towns and Rockaways is thriving with more than 1,400 students from preschool through high school. Here, the elementary school boys are seen marching in the Salute to Israel Parade in 2009. (Courtesy of the *Jewish Star*.)

Rabbi Shlomo Freifeld had a big personality. His influence changed the face of the Far Rockaway Community and essentially the entire Five Towns. He established a vibrant outreach yeshiva in Far Rockaway in 1967, influencing thousands of students who either attended his classes or met him for a few short hours. He was a pioneering figure in the baal teshuva movement throughout the 1970s and 1980s. Rabbi Shlomo Freifeld was born in 1925 in East New York and attended Yeshiva Toras Chaim elementary and Chaim Berlin High School and Post High School, where he became a close disciple of Rabbi Isaac Hutner. (Courtesy of Yitzchok Halperin.)

After a position in Toronto, Rabbi Freifeld returned to Chaim Berlin, which had relocated from Brooklyn to Far Rockaway, but when Chaim Berlin moved back to Brooklyn, Rabbi Freifeld chose to remain in Far Rockaway and founded Sh'or Yoshuv, a yeshiva that accepted any young man who wanted to study Torah. Rabbi Freifeld's nonjudgmental approach to teaching Torah attracted many students from a wide variety of Jewish backgrounds. As the Far Rockaway community began to fall victim to crime, Rabbi Freifeld's students held fast and remained loyal to the community, promoting stability that served the future growth of the Far Rockaway community. Rabbi Friefeld passed away at the young age of 65 in 1990. (Courtesy of Yitzchok Halperin.)

Rabbi Freifeld's two sons-in-law, Rabbi Avraham Halperin and Rabbi Naftali Jaeger, help lead the yeshiva through their dynamic personalities. Shown here is Rabbi Halperin teaching a group of newcomers to the yeshiva. (Courtesy of Yitzchok Halperin.)

Rabbi Naftali Jaeger, a renowned Torah scholar, continues to lead the yeshiva in their spacious new facility on a multiacre campus in Lawrence, New York. He is seen here lecturing to advanced students and community members. (Courtesy of Yitzchok Halperin.)

112

The original building of Sh'or Yoshov Central Avenue was originally the Riverside Funeral Home of Far Rockaway. As the yeshiva grew, every room was utilized. The inside of the study hall was originally the mortuary. (Courtesy of Yitzchok Halperin.)

Seen here is the cramped inside of the building where the Talmudic students would bask in the glow of their dynamic rebbe. Subsequently, the yeshiva bought a building a half mile west on Central Avenue and named it in memory of David Miller, of Woodmere, a longtime supporter of the yeshiva. In 2003, the yeshiva moved to a spacious new campus in Lawrence, New York, that includes several buildings servicing hundreds of students that come from the Metropolitan area as well as from across the United States and all corners of the globe. (Courtesy of Yitzchok Halperin.)

In the late 1970s, Rabbi Freifeld instructed his student Rabbi Dovid Sitnick to open a small childrens' yeshiva to be called Talmud Torah Siach Yitzchok. The mission, according to Rabbi Freifeld, was "to create an environment where Torah is learned in its purest form—that is unyielding to the outside forces that permeate our present-day surroundings." An old synagogue led by Rabbi Yehuda Mashitz whose membership was dwindling was purchased and renovated. It now educates more than 250 children. (Both, courtesy of Yitzchok Halperin.)

Four

JEWISH COMMUNITY LIFE AND PERSONALITIES

The Five Towns enjoyed a rich Jewish life, with many rituals becoming major communal events. As sacred Jewish texts may not be disposed of indiscriminately, the tradition of burying worn out or tattered sacred Jewish books is often done at a ground breaking or foundation pouring, as a pit is dug for their final resting place. Here, four Rabbis from four communities join together to bury *shaimos* (torn or tattered) pages of holy books. From left to right are unidentified, Rabbi Sidney Lebor, of Young Israel of Woodmere; Rabbi Moshe Chait, of Young Israel of Wavecrest and Bayswater; and Rabbi Nuchim Kornmehl of Young Israel Lawrence-Cedarhurst.

At the 1965 bar mitzvah of Marvin Goldstein are, from right to left, Marvin Goldstein, Jody Bergman, Michael Litton, Sam Friedman, unidentified, Allen Greenberg, and Heshy Marcus. (Courtesy of Adele Goldstein.)

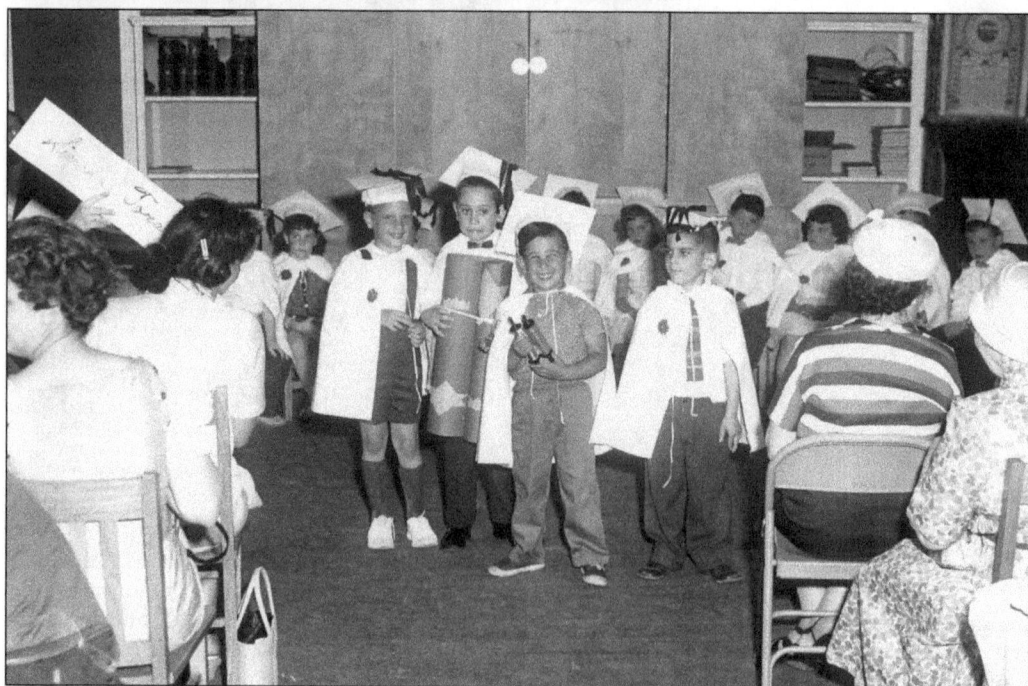

Kindergarten graduations were joyous occasions especially for children of survivors or escapees from Nazi Germany. Some of the children at this 1962 graduation grew up to be prominent doctors, attorneys, and leaders in their respective communities. (Courtesy of Adele Goldstein.)

Kosher and kosher-style food has always been part and parcel of the Five Towns. Toddy's appetizers was established in 1946, and although it was an icon in the community established by the Toddman family, it did not cater to the Orthodox population. In 1987, Toddy's decided to close on Saturday and come under the strict supervision of the Orthodox Vaad of Kashrus. According to Jay Toddman, the Sabbath closing of Toddy's was not born of Orthodox coercion but was merely a good business decision to attract the growing number of customers who wanted strictly kosher food according to the standards of the supervising agency. (Courtesy of the Long Island Collection at Hofstra University.)

Sabra Kosher Pizza originally opened in 1966 on Mott Avenue in Far Rockaway as the first kosher pizza store in the Five Towns and Far Rockaway area by Joseph "ZuZu" and Ruthie Barnes. In 1974, it moved to Cedarhurst's Central Avenue, as one of the first kosher eateries in the area. It was sold after the passing of Ruthie Barnes and closed its doors after 41 years on February 18, 2013. Stores like Burger Nosh, a kosher fast-food burger joint, and other fast-food types eventually followed. Soon, upscale restaurants like Chosen Island (a kosher Chinese restaurant) and Abigails followed suit. Today, there are dozens of kosher eateries in the Five Towns, and patrons come from all parts of the metro area to enjoy. (Courtesy of the Long Island Collection at Hofstra University.)

The Young Israel of Woodmere established a Sabbath-observant Little League team in the mid-1960s. The team would only play on Sundays or weekdays and competed with teams from synagogues throughout the area and were coached by members of the synagogue's men's club. Unlike the current Little League teams in today's Orthodox league, the players wore real uniforms and spiked shoes. From left to right are (first row) Noam Marans, Zvi Kamenetzky, Ezra Friedlander, unidentified, Arthur Luxenberg, Mordechai Kamenetzky, and David Bodek; (second row) Ira Heller, unidentified, Maury Heller, Zvi Marans, Billy Eisenberg, William Hochman, Howard Friedman, unidentified, Ellie Libin, Fred Schulman, and unidentified; (third row) coaches Irwin Luxenberg, Morris Hochman, unidentified, and Emanuel Libin.

In addition to baseball teams, synagogues created Jewish basketball teams so that every member could have a chance for his children to play even if they were not qualified for high school varsity basketball. Many of the games were more pickup types with some players not wearing uniforms or sneakers. The Shaaray Tefila basketball team is pictured in the 1960s. (Courtesy of Congregation Shaaray Tefila.)

Notable personalities, philanthropists, politicians, and community activists have always been found in Far Rockaway and the Five Towns. Together, they have made an impact not only locally regarding issues that affect the area but also globally in relation to national and world events, particularly regarding the State of Israel. Pictured, George Blumenthal discusses the formation of the Israel Cancer Research Foundation with Dr. Yashar Hirshaut, a noted oncologist who became president and chairman of the foundation. From left to right are George Blumenthal, Steven Kevelson, Dr. Yashar Hirshaut, and Rabbi Benjamin Kamenetzky.

The Five Towns Jewish community was actively involved with politicians on a broad level, from local politicians to the national scene. Pictured from left to right are Nassau County Republican leader Peter DeSibio, Congressman Raymond McGrath, Nassau County executive Thomas Gullota, and Rabbi Benjamin Kamenetzky.

Dr. Yashar Hirshaut and his wife, Perry, moved to the Lawrence area in the mid-1970s. They became known for their open house for all in need. Dr. Hirshaut, a board-certified oncologist in New York, is a relentless patient advocate, advisor, and friend to hundreds who sought his advice and expertise in the field of medical oncology.

Milton and Molly Schulman arrived a short time after the founding of the first minyan but became actively involved in every part of communal life in the Five Towns. The owner of ABC Hanger and Supply Company, which sold fixtures to the retail industry, Milton was a generous supporter of Young Israel, Yeshiva of South Shore, and Ohel Family Services. Their children Robert, Howard, and Fred are all involved in communal affairs, with Fred being the head of the Chevra Kadisha the Jewish burial society of the White Shul. The family is pictured in front of their home at 23 Park Circle in 1956 going to Robert's bar mitzvah. From left to right are Robert Schulman, Howard Schulman, Mollie Schulman, and Milton Schulman. (Fred was born in 1957.) (Courtesy of the Schulman family.)

Frank Herman (pictured far right) was originally born in Hungary in 1908 to a well-established family in the lumber business. He was his community's president before the invasion of the Nazis, and at the start of the invasion he used his influence to save many of his fellow Jews. He survived the war and came to America, moving to Five Towns Orthodox community. A founding member of Young Israel of Woodmere, he was instrumental in providing funding for the new building. He later moved to Lawrence and became active in the growth of Congregation Beth Sholom.

Harry Walker, the founder of the speakers' agency that represented former presidents and many other celebrities, was active in communal life in the Five Towns and Rockaways in the role he played in the building of synagogues and yeshivas. After graduating from Yeshiva University, he earned a master's degree in social work from the Jewish Institute of Religion and was hired as the executive director of the Jewish Community Center of Quincy, Massachusetts.

There is hardly an institution in the Five Towns that was developed during the 1950s through the 1970s whose success was not bolstered by the support and influence of Herbert Tenzer. Despite his association with the world of politics and secular culture, Congressman Tenzer (NYS 5th Congressional District, 1965–1969) had a powerful feel for Orthodox Judaism and for Torah study. He was instrumental in the founding of the Albert Einstein College of Medicine and the Benjamin N. Cardozo School of Law at Yeshiva University. He was the president of the Crown Heights Yeshiva and the president of Congregation Beth Sholom. He was an ardent spokesman for Torah and Orthodox Jewry.

Dr. Manfred Lehmann was the president of Lehmann Trading Corporation, an international trading firm founded by his father in 1904. He was also the founder of the Intergovernmental Philatelic Corporation. Recognizing the importance of emerging African nations since the 1950s, he, as well as his wife, Anne, was actively involved with Ghana, Togo, Dahomey (now Benin), Kenya, Tanzania, Uganda, Somalia, Bahamas, Trinidad, Grenada, Antigua, Marshall Islands, and Palau, among others. In addition to being a successful businessman, political activist, and world traveler, Dr. Lehmann was an esteemed scholar who published prolifically. The Lehmanns' influence and philanthropy helped found and perpetuate Young Israel of Woodmere, Young Israel of Lawrence-Cedarhurst, and Yeshiva of South Shore, among others. The campus of Yeshiva of South Shore is named for him and his son Jamie, who passed away at an early age. (Courtesy of the Lehmann family.)

George and Rose Blumenthal's interest in the growth of the greater Five Towns and Rockaways Jewish community knew no bounds. He was chairman of the building committee at the White Shul; a board member of HILI, which helped purchase Camp HILI in White Lake, New York, as a summer retreat for children; and a builder and supporter of Rabbi Dovid Speigel's shteeble synagogue in Cedarhurst and Rabbi Kamenetzky's Yeshiva in Woodmere, where his son R. Dean (pictured second row, second from left) continues to be heavily involved as an active member and supporter. (Courtesy of R. Dean Blumenthal.)

Morris Morgenstern grew up on the Lower East Side and became a successful financier and philanthropist who contributed to numerous causes, Jewish and non-Jewish. He moved to Woodmere in the 1940s and donated generously to local synagogues and yeshivas as well as cultural and social institutions in the area. In 1949, he established the Morris Morgenstern Foundation to provide financial aid to religious, educational, and charitable institutions of all faiths. Morris Morgenstern owned several important historical documents, among them George Washington's famous letter to the Touro Synagogue of Newport, Rhode Island, which included the phrase "to bigotry no sanction, to persecution no assistance." Morris Morgenstern passed away on June 9, 1969. He is pictured here presenting a plaque to Dr. Jonas Salk, who discovered the polio vaccine.

Velvel Pasternak, the son of Polish immigrants, is a Toronto-born musicologist, conductor, arranger, producer, and publisher of Jewish music. He studied at Yeshiva University and Juilliard and holds a master's degree in music education at Columbia. An expert on Hasidic music and one of the first producers of Hasidic records, Pasternak taught music at Hillel, Brandeis, and the Yeshiva of South Shore, among others. His Cedarhurst-based Tara Publications has been responsible for the publication of 26 recordings and over 150 books of Jewish music since 1971, spanning the gamut of Israeli, Yiddish, Ladino, cantorial, Hasidic, and Holocaust music. He is a regular lecturer on the music of the Hasidim. Pasternak plays the role of author, publisher, record producer, distributor and salesman of wares that find their way to thousands of Jewish music lovers throughout the world. He is pictured below around 1966 with the Yeshiva of South Shore choir. (Courtesy of Arthur Elfenbein.)

Myron Kaufman is a successful developer and principal of the Basser Kaufman Realty Group with holdings across the northeastern portion of the United States. A native of Far Rockaway, he grew up in the shadow of Congregation of Shaaray Tefila. Kaufman bought the original land for the Young Israel of Woodmere for thousands of dollars yet sold it back to them for $1, enabling the young shul to kick start what would become exponential growth.

Robert and Estelle Schwartz were philanthropists who lived in Hewlett Bay Park. Robert and his brothers owned Paragon Oil, which continued in operation until the late 1950s. At that point, the brothers were getting older and wished to retire. The company was sold to Texaco in the late 1950s, at an estimated sale price in excess of $75 million. The Schwartzes, residents of Woodmere, contributed to many institutions, including the Metropolitan Opera at the newly built Lincoln Center, to New York University, Mt. Sinai Hospital, Fifth Avenue Synagogue, and Yeshiva of South Shore. Seen here are Robert and Estelle Schwartz, standing with Rabbi Benjamin Kamenetzky (far left) in front of a plaque commemorating their benevolence.

127

Visit us at
arcadiapublishing.com

www.ingramcontent.com/pod-product-compliance
Lightning Source LLC
Chambersburg PA
CBHW050639110426
42813CB00007B/1862